SPAIN'S ENTRY INTO NATO

SPAIN'S ENTRY INTO NATO

Conflicting Political and Strategic Perspectives

edited by
Federico G. Gil
Joseph S. Tulchin

Lynne Rienner Publishers • Boulder & London

Published in the United States of America in 1988 by
Lynne Rienner Publishers, Inc.
948 North Street, Boulder, Colorado 80302

and in the United Kingdom by
Lynne Rienner Publishers, Inc.
3 Henrietta Street, Covent Garden, London WC2E 8LU

©1988 by Lynne Rienner Publishers, Inc. All rights reserved

Library of Congress Cataloging-in-Publication Data

Spain's entry into NATO : conflicting political and strategic
perspectives / edited by Federico G. Gil and Joseph S. Tulchin.

Papers presented at the fourth in a series of conferences
sponsored by the University of North Carolina at Chapel Hill in
cooperation with the Instituto de Cooperación Iberoamericana and the
Centro de Investigaciones Sociológicas.

Includes index.
ISBN 1-55587-117-8
 1. North Atlantic Treaty Organization—Spain—Congresses.
2. Spain—Military policy—Congresses.   3. Spain—History—1975–
—Congresses.   I. Gil, Federico Guillermo.   II. Tulchin, Joseph S.,
1939– .   III. University of North Carolina at Chapel Hill.
IV. Instituto de Cooperación Iberoamericana (Madrid, Spain)
V. Centro de Investigaciones Sociológicas.
UA646.5.S7S63   1988   88-4973
355'.033046—dc19   CIP

British Library Cataloguing in Publication Data
A Cataloguing in Publication record for this book
is available from the British Library.

Printed and bound in the United States of America

The paper used in this publication meets
the requirements of the American National
Standard for Permanence of Paper for
Printed Library Materials Z39.48-1984.

Contents

Acknowledgments	vi
Contributors	vii
Introduction, *Federico G. Gil and Joseph S. Tulchin*	1

Part 1 SPANISH POLITICAL PERSPECTIVES ON NATO

1. The Transition to Democracy and Spain's Membership in NATO, *Javier Tusell*	11
2. Repercussions on the Democratic Process of Spain's Entry into NATO, *Javier Pérez Royo*	20
3. Spanish Media and the Two NATO Campaigns, *Inocencio Félix Arias*	29
4. Spain, A Singular Ally, *Joaquín Abril Martorell*	41

Part 2 SPANISH FOREIGN POLICY, THE UNITED STATES, AND THE WESTERN ALLIANCE

5. Atlanticism and Europeanism: NATO and Trends in Spanish Foreign Policy, *Emilio A. Rodríguez*	55
6. European Community Enlargement and the Evolution of French-Spanish Cooperation, 1977–1987, *Glen D. Macdonald*	72

Part 3 STRATEGIC IMPLICATIONS OF SPAIN'S ENTRY INTO NATO

7. European Socialism, the Western Alliance, and Central America: Lost Latin American Illusions, *Carlos Rico F.*	95
8. Spain, the United States, and NATO: Strategic Facts and Political Realities, *Gregory F. Treverton*	122
9. Spain in NATO: The Reluctant Partner, *Glenn H. Snyder*	140
10. Epilogue, *Joseph S. Tulchin*	159
Index	173
About the Book and the Editors	179

Acknowledgments

We want to thank the participants in the open discussions following each session of the conference at Chapel Hill, out of which this book grew, for drawing our attention to the points of contact between the differing perspectives represented in the papers. Their comments helped the authors improve their papers and opened several new subjects for future discussion. Those who gave the benefit of their insights during the conference were: Jack Donnelly III, James R. Leutze, Ubaldo Martínez, Pilar Saro y Saro, Lars Schoultz, and Samuel R. Williamson, Jr. In addition, thanks are due the Comité Conjunto for providing travel funds for the Spanish participants and for making possible the Spanish edition of this book. The College of Arts and Sciences and the Office of International Programs also provided generous support. The Institute of Latin American Studies, with Lars Schoultz, Director, and Sharon Mújica, Administrative Assistant, provided all manner of support—financial, moral, and organizational. In the Instituto de Cooperación Iberoamericana (ICI), María Carmen Ordóñez was of inestimable help. We are grateful to them all and to the authorities of the sponsoring institutions whose confidence and backing have kept the Convenio alive.

Federico G. Gil
Joseph S. Tulchin
Chapel Hill, April 1988

Contributors

Joaquin Abril Martorell, president, Comisión de Relaciones Exteriores, Cámara de Diputados

Inocencio Félix Arias, director, Oficina de Información Diplomática, Ministerio de Relaciones Exteriores

Federico G. Gil, Kenan Professor of Political Science, Emeritus, The University of North Carolina

Glen D. Macdonald, Ford Fellow, Center of International Affairs, Harvard University

Javier Pérez Royo, professor of constitutional law, Universidad de Sevilla

Carlos Rico F., director, North American studies, Instituto Latinoamericano de Estudios Transnacionales, Mexico; senior researcher, el Collegio de Mexico

Emilio A. Rodríguez, assistant professor of political science, University of South Alabama

Glenn H. Snyder, professor of political science, The University of North Carolina

Gregory F. Treverton, professor of public policy, John F. Kennedy School of Government, Harvard University

Joseph S. Tulchin, professor of history, director of the Office of International Programs, The University of North Carolina

Javier Tusell, professor of contemporary history, Universidad Nacional de Educación a Distancia

Introduction

Federico G. Gil and Joseph S. Tulchin

Spain's role in NATO is a subject of intense concern in Spain and throughout Europe. Because of its obvious military and strategic implications, and because it is significant also for the evolving definition of Spain's reinsertion in world affairs after forty years of isolation, the subject is inextricably linked to the politically sensitive bilateral negotiations over U.S. bases on Spanish territory. Those negotiations, which at this writing have yet to be concluded, are charged with references to Spain's enforced alienation from the international community during the dictatorship of Francisco Franco.

When the options were presented in dichotomous terms, Spain had to join NATO, just as it had to join the European Community. There was no other viable option. In the transition to democracy after Franco's death in 1975, those in charge of the government felt it imperative to declare the nation's European commitment and its adherence to Western values. In so doing, they hoped to speed the reintegration of Spain into the international community. The vast majority of the Spanish public supported those general objectives. On the more specific question of joining NATO, the Spanish public was—and is—painfully divided.

The confusion in Spanish public opinion is of long gestation and reflects the historical experience of the Spanish people and the ambiguities of their leaders on questions of international affairs. Spain did not participate in World War II, nor in the postwar tensions of the cold war. Because of their isolation from the formative experiences of the current generation, East and West, Spaniards have little appreciation of the visceral questions of international politics; they cannot understand the nightmares of their European allies that explain so much of their foreign policies.

But the confusion in Spanish public opinion stems not only from the lack of shared experiences, it also involves conflicting messages from Spain's own historical experience. Franco's anticommunism never was in doubt. Nevertheless, it was the Western democracies, uniting after the war in their opposition to the Soviet Union and to communist subversion of their governments, that declared Spain the pariah of the West. Franco responded to the exclusion from the United Nations with a public campaign emphasizing the virtues of Spanish nationalism and the macho strength of the Spanish people. Posters proclaimed, "Ellos tienen UNO. Nosotros tenemos Dos." Even when the United States finally bowed to the logic of its own national security policy in 1953, and granted Franco international legitimacy through the defense treaties, the dictator covered his nationalist flank by stimulating the latent anti-Americanism among the Spanish people.

He did so by playing on two historical sources of bitterness toward the United States. One, on the political Left, remembered that only the Soviet Union had come to the aid of the Republic during the Civil War, while the Western democracies, including the United States, sat on their hands watching Nazi Germany and Fascist Italy provide Franco with the support he needed to destroy the Republic. For this group, the defense treaties and the bases were another demonstration that the democracies were either hypocritical or not very democratic. The group on the Right drew their historical inspiration from the disastrous war with the United States in 1898. For them, the United States represented an insensitive, imperialistic, materialistic force that ran counter to the values of Spanish tradition, to *Hispanidad*. The presence of U.S. bases on Spanish soil, for them, was another demonstration that the United States was not sensitive to their national concerns. In public opinion polls from the early 1960s to the present, strong feelings of hostility to the United States appear all across the political spectrum, with particular virulence on the far Right, the far Left, and among the devoutly Catholic. Today, when asked which of the superpowers, the United States or the USSR, represents the greater threat to world peace, the Spanish people are split in half. Given the configuration of Spanish public opinion on these issues, no wonder the political leadership of the nation is unwilling or unable to define its position with clarity!

In the face of such doubt and ambiguity, it is logical to ask the question, "Why did Spain join NATO?" The answer is that there was—and is—no viable option. It was considered part of the inevitable process of rejoining the European mainstream. All political groups believe that Spain is a Western nation. To reject NATO, to spurn the EEC, would be to perpetuate the marginalization that was an integral part of the Franco experience. No responsible politician wants to do that. So, Spain pushes ahead toward reintegration into the Western community. As it does, it must resolve four clusters of issues or problems that create tension with the Western allies and, especially, with the United States. These issues are: (1) the definition of strategic concerns; (2) the nature of Spain's participation in the alliance; (3) the severe asymmetry of foreign policy priorities between the United States and Spain; and (4) Spain's special relationship with Latin America.

For a variety of reasons—historical, geographical, and cultural—Spain defines its strategic concerns differently from its NATO allies. Spain is deeply concerned with a threat from the south, from the Mahgreb. The enclaves of Ceuta and Melilla are vulnerable, and the Balearic and Canary islands are virtually undefended. The revindication of Gibraltar is an imperative of Spanish nationalism. Spain insists that any alliance of which it is a part must take these threats into account. Thus far, it has had a difficult time getting the allies to recognize them. By the same token, many people in Spain simply do not consider the Soviet Union as a threat to the nation's security. Indeed, many groups, on the Left and on the Right, consider the bipolar struggle a product of U.S. hegemonic hubris and feel it would dissipate or disappear if that hegemony were moderated.

Given these fundamental differences of perspective, it is not surprising that Spain's entry into NATO has occasioned complicated negotiations often characterized by high levels of tension. The critics of Spain's posture accuse it of being semialigned, or a "cheap rider" within the alliance, charges the Spanish government vehemently denies. There is no question that the addition of Spain will change NATO, just as the Gaullist option and the addition of Greece or Turkey changed it. It is to be hoped that Spain will bring new ideas to the alliance as well as a fresh perspective on old problems. Spain comes to NATO at a critical time. It is a time of transition from a period of clear domination by the United States to one of shared influence among the allies and one that will be marked by increasing responsibilities outside of Europe. The recent signing of the treaty reducing intermediate range missiles, between the United States and the USSR, will increase the importance of conventional forces and of strategic bases.

The changes in NATO have caused considerable disquiet to the United States. The question of responsibility for European and Western security is a complex and sensitive one. From the perspective of the U.S. government, the bases in Spain are only one piece in a large puzzle. Officials in Washington consider that the Spanish demands for a reduction in troop levels in Spain come at a particularly unfortunate time. Moreover, they believe that the Spanish demands must be evaluated within the context of the security requirements of the alliance. Of course, for Spain, the bases issue is a question of national sovereignty and a matter of the highest importance. The latest round of negotiations between the two governments has exposed in Spanish public opinion and foreign policy a glaring asymmetry of priorities between the importance of the United States and of the bases, as compared with the low priority of Spain and the bases in U.S. public opinion and foreign policy.

This asymmetry compounds the difficulties inherent in the talks, and complicates the entire gamut of relations between the two countries. Worse, it means that senior officials in Washington, notably ex-Secretary Caspar Weinberger and Secretary George Schultz, have very little patience with Spain, and little concern to be sensitive to the idiosyncrasies of Spain's role in world affairs. Their disposition to listen attentively to Spanish arguments is not enhanced by attacks in the U.S. Congress against Spanish threats to close U.S. bases, a position the Spanish government never has assumed. American cabinet members are not comfortable when foreign policy issues become distorted in the peculiar arena of U.S. domestic politics. The Spanish government is anxious to resolve the talks amicably but there is a real danger that the asymmetry of relations between the two nations and differences in their perspectives on strategic issues will push the Spanish to a more extreme posture than they would like to assume and reduce to the vanishing point the capacity of U.S. officials to deal sympathetically with such a posture. This danger was diminished, though not eliminated, when the U.S. agreed in January 1988 to close the air base at Torrejón.

The special relationship Spain claims to have with Latin America exacerbates tensions with the United States. It represents a potential dilution or at least a confusion of U.S. influence or hegemony in the hemisphere. This is especially true in moments, such as the present, when the U.S. government insists on defining the situation in Central America in terms of its national security. This means that interposition by Spain, even in the form of friendly mediation, is seen by the Reagan administration as noisome meddling or, at best, an inconvenient annoyance. Further, the attempt by Spain to give substance to its special relationship with Latin America by raising the sensitivity of its European colleagues to Latin American problems serves inevitably to emphasize the unorthodox nature, even the deviance, of Spain's participation in the Western alliance. Of course, from the official Spanish perspective, the heterodoxy of its positions is a virtue, a strength. The president of the Spanish government, Felipe González, has reiterated on many occasions that Spain has to bring new ideas to NATO and to the European Community. Recent experiences suggest that, while new ideas are very badly needed, they are not always received with enthusiasm by Spain's new partners.

* * *

In this book, we have tried to contribute to a better understanding of the Spanish position in NATO and, more generally, in world affairs. We believe we have shed considerable light as well on the bilateral relationship between Spain and the United States.

The genesis of the book lay in a conference at Chapel Hill, the fourth under the Convenio between the University of North Carolina and the Instituto de Cooperación Iberoamericana and the Centro de Investigaciones Sociológicas. The conference was designed to define the issues confronting Spain and the issues which Spain's relatively recent reinsertion into the European Community represent for the entire Western community, especially the United States. By juxtaposing papers from differing Spanish political perspectives, the nature of the internal debate was defined. By juxtaposing Spanish perspectives with strategic and political perspectives typical of the United States and the Western bloc, the nexus of issues complicating Spain's reinsertion into the European Community was thrown into high relief.

We have organized the book into three parts. In the first, Javier Tusell emphasizes the importance of putting the process of Spain's entry into NATO in the context of the country's recent historical experience. He talks about the relationship of the political parties to the foreign policy decisions, but gives more attention to attitudes and perceptions than to matters of partisan strategy. His focus is on why and how Spain entered NATO when it did, though he is in agreement with Pérez Royo (Chapter 2) concerning the political opportunism involved in calling the referendum and concerning its harmful consequences for Spanish political institutions. Tusell is more attentive to ideology than the other analysts and is especially critical of the lack of ideological clarity in the process of public debate surrounding the issue of NATO in Spain.

Beginning with considerations about "direct democracy" in the comparative context of contemporary European politics, Javier Pérez

Royo discusses the evolution of attitudes toward the referendum within the various parties, with most attention to the Partido Socialista Obrero Español (PSOE). He recognizes that the outbound government of Calvo Sotelo forced the decision on the PSOE, but believes that the PSOE then used the referendum to strengthen itself politically while weakening Spain's fragile representative institutions.

When the Socialists called the referendum, argues Pérez Royo, the decision to join NATO was already irreversible, so that the referendum's only real function was as a plebiscite from the Socialist government. The harm it did, on the other hand, was considerable. The acerbic climate of the referendum campaign brought out an authoritarian streak within the PSOE and a mistrustful public attitude toward the government. Felipe González made the referendum a personal issue and, according to Pérez Royo, the campaign reinforced troublesome personalist tendencies in Spanish politics. The referendum accentuated the crisis of the Right, which had its natural "pro-Western" position usurped by the PSOE. Most importantly, the referendum took an important political process out of the institutional channels which it is in Spain's best interest to keep in use.

Inocencio Félix Arias offers a detailed analysis of the mass media and the public opinion polls during the two campaigns dealing with NATO. He demonstrates how the equivocal attitude of the Suárez government in the first campaign (1981-1982) and the decided posture of the González government in the second (1985-1986) had different impacts on the public. His summary demonstrates that in the second campaign it became clear toward the end that a negative vote was inconceivable, and that stimulated a last-minute stampede to support the government and NATO.

Joaquín Abril Martorell presents the origins of things—of Spanish attitudes, of NATO, of the problems between them. Though Abril Martorell, the politician, avoids partisan comments, Pérez Royo and Tussell, both academics, are critical of the PSOE government's handling of the affairs. His version of the history of the cold war supports the point made by Snyder (Chapter 9) that Spain is a semialigned nation.

In the second part, Emilo A. Rodríguez focuses on the tension Spain experiences between its European option and its Atlantic option, given its historical links to Latin America. He sees a dialectic between these two options since Franco's death. Ties to the United States are part of the Atlantic option. He argues that the PSOE government has used membership in NATO as a tool to maximize integration into Europe and as an aid in bilateral dealings with the

United States. He feels the change in the PSOE position on NATO was the result of an internal split and concludes that the González government has balanced its commitments to Europe and to Latin America.

Glen D. Macdonald stresses the links between domestic politics and foreign policy and between economics and security issues in the bilateral relations between France and Spain. He divides the relations between the two nations since the defeat of Franco into three phases, which he calls the diagnostic (1976-1982), formula (1983-1984), and institutionalization (1985-1987) phases. While he admits there are important external constraints on French-Spanish cooperation, he is convinced that the strong improvement in bilateral relations in the last few years is due more to changes in the internal regimes of the two nations than to any other factor.

In the first chapter of Part III, Carlos Rico F., by describing the recent history of the role of European social democratic movements in Central America, simultaneously explains the dilemma of Spain's Socialist government in its dealings with the United States and sheds considerable light on the Spanish desire to demonstrate its special relationship to its former colonies in the Western Hemisphere. Rico puts the efforts of the European social democrats to mediate the conflicts on the isthmus into the context of European politics on the one hand and, on the other, into the context of Latin American efforts to free themselves, if only partially, from the stranglehold on their affairs wielded by the United States. While Rico does not focus exclusively on Spain's hemispheric dilemma, his essay helps us to understand why Spain's relationship with NATO and with the West is so complicated.

Gregory F. Treverton emphasizes that the nature of Spain's participation in NATO is tied closely to the issue of the U.S. bases in Spain. He takes a realistic view of the alliance's military requirements and concludes that the allies really expect very little from Spain in the short run. Spain is not yet significant to U.S. military planners. The bases negotiations are important to the United States as a potentially dangerous precedent for other allies who might want to reduce the U.S. presence at a time or in a manner not convenient to the United States and to the other allies.

Glenn H. Snyder's is the most theoretical chapter in the entire book. Snyder puts Spain's heterodox participation in NATO into comparative perspective and offers a discussion of the "cheap rider" phenomenon in alliances. On the basis of his comparative analysis, Snyder suggests that Spain's alignment status will be determined by domestic political issues because of the absence of external constraints, because it is geographically farthest from the defined threat, and because it is the latest to enter the alliance.

In the final chapter, Joseph S. Tulchin knits together the various strands presented in the preceeding chapters. He explores the conflicting pressures of Spanish public opinion and explains how these pressures, together with U.S. perceptions of Spanish initiatives in the Western Hemisphere, have complicated bilateral negotiations over renewing the bases agreement. These complications have severely strained Spain's growing ties to NATO. To limit the potential damage, Spain is expanding its activities in the Economic Community and in NATO meetings. On the U.S. side, because of the low salience of Spanish issues in U.S. politics, personalities played an unusually important role in the bilateral talks, which made a compromise settlement harder to achieve.

PART 1
SPANISH POLITICAL PERSPECTIVES ON NATO

1

The Transition to Democracy and Spain's Membership in NATO

Javier Tusell

The Spanish transition to democracy has habitually been considered an exemplary and unprecedented process in which dictatorial political institutions were transformed into democratic ones. This favorable judgment is doubtless correct. The democratization of Spanish political institutions was done at the least social cost and with much less risk than in Portugal, to cite an example near at hand, even though the duration of the dictatorship and the existence of grave conflicts in several areas seemed to augur greater difficulties. Nonetheless, the most negative aspect of this transition is seldom taken into account: its temporally boundless, indefinite, indeed almost infinite character. This is to say that, having accomplished the fundamentals of the transition in a relatively short time, Spain has advanced more slowly in its homologation to Western European patterns of public opinion and political behavior. Such a situation was to be expected, and the gradual decanting of Spain into the new mold remains, until now, incomplete and characteristically Spanish. For example, it would appear that the system of political parties is not fully consolidated. This pattern of successive homologation is particularly clear in Spanish foreign policy, more concretely, in Spain's political, economic, and above all, military links with its Western European neighbors. Here the decanting into a new mold has been so self-evident as to merit little discussion. The conduct of Spain's relationship with NATO has been distinguished by the greatest errors committed by the dominant political class in the whole process of democratic transition.

Things would not have been so were it not for some very peculiar circumstances of the Spanish case. The contemporary history of Spain has been characterized by a general absence of popular consensus concerning internal political organization, and this has inevitably modified foreign policy as well. When people affirm a Spanish tradition of neutrality they overlook the real origins of that neutrality in contemporary Spain. It was a neutrality born of impotence, impotence which itself sprang from a lack of the most minimal agreement on internal political matters. Neutrality was the policy of the Spanish state, but hardly of Spanish parties and social organizations which were absolutely belligerent in outlook during both world wars.

The situation was accentuated by the dictatorial regime that came to power in 1939. In its relations with other Western European countries, Spain was to experience an anomalous situation which can be summed up in two terms: a will to be different, and an "obligatory introversion." Of these, the will to be different was the most basic factor. It was inevitable since it supposedly justified Spain's peculiar dictatorial institutions. As for the introversion, it too was inevitable since the Western powers never dealt as equals with Franco's Spain precisely because of those very peculiarities. Forced by strategic necessities stemming from the country's geographic position, Western powers finally sought pacts with Spain, but they were quasi-colonial in tone and, as Marquina has said, they were negotiated "through the back door." The bilateral relations established in 1953 granted NATO an extensive role in Spanish defense. Spain was considered a "vital element" in U.S. strategy, but the arrangement deprived Spaniards of any important voice in decisions that affected their interests. Though it changed with time, Spain's place in Western defensive strategy remained key, and its role in the planning of that strategy remained subordinate because of the dictatorial nature of its political institutions under Franco.

Thus, the recent historical experience of the Spanish people has been far different from that of other Western Europeans. The cold war could not be presented in terms of a communist menace to Spanish democratic institutions since Spain had none. In fact, Franco's constant appeal to a communist threat sometimes even equated communism and democracy. U.S. soldiers did not arrive in Spain to liberate the Spanish people from fascism but rather seemed to support Franco's dictatorship, if only for military reasons.

These considerations explain certain attitudes of the political class at the beginning of the transition to democracy. The moderate opposition in exile had identified itself with the cause of NATO. Indalecio Prieto and Rodolfo Llopis, principal Socialist leaders, asserted repeatedly that a democratic Spain ought to join NATO. At the time, their position was similar to that of other European socialists like Bevin, who played an important part in the creation of the NATO alliance, but the Spanish Socialist position was to change markedly. In 1972 the Socialist party was transformed by the triumph within its ranks of young, radical members who rejected strategic alignment with the West. By 1976 the party took the view that the U.S. military bases compromised Spanish sovereignty and ought to be dismantled. In 1977 Felipe González's trip to Moscow confirmed the Socialist policy of nonalignment. In 1980 the Socialist Party proposed the removal of nuclear arms and the creation of a neutral zone in the Mediterranean. With the passage of time, the Socialist position had evolved from support for NATO to what Javier Rupérez called a "theological attitude" of condemnation which associated NATO with militarism and viewed it as an obstacle to the creation of a socialist society.

Significantly, other political groups in Spain were at least obliquely supportive of the Socialist position at the time. Formerly orthodox Franquistas adopted attitudes much more favorable to bilateral relations with the United States than to joining NATO (the position of Carrero Blanco). This may have influenced Adolfo Suárez himself, but other groupings in his party not of Franquista origin also showed an initial reticence to the idea of joining NATO. Javier Rupérez himself, later the first Spanish ambassador to NATO, admits to some such reservations during the early stages of the democratization process. The position taken by Suárez obviously responded to the prevalence of such attitudes and to fundamental priorities in internal political affairs, which absorbed his attention. The question of Spain's entry into NATO might have provoked a deep split in the political class during the debates surrounding the writing of the new constitution. In any case, the policy of the centrist governments well deserved the labels "zigzagging" and "ambiguous," and some aspects of Suárez's management of the affair are less defensible. It is doubtful how the NATO card could be played to advantage in the Spanish negotiation with the European Community (EC). Above all, Suárez made such show of acumen and a supposed sixth sense that he appeared at times bereft of practical information on the conduct of foreign policy. It is clear that he remained limited by the parameters of foreign policy in the Spain of years past. Possibly he also feared that joining NATO could have destabilizing repercussions for the country's fledgling democracy if it led to terrorist reprisals. But the policies he followed were quite contradictory. He combined a democratic internal political line with diplomatic embraces for Yasir Arafat and Fidel Castro. Spanish representatives attended the Conference of Unaligned Nations but protested stridently there when Castro recommended that Spain not enter NATO. Most likely, nobody took Suárez's foreign policy very seriously on this point at all; he succeeded only in making other countries wary, and he failed utterly to establish the autonomy of Spanish foreign policy which it was his purpose to exhibit. In any case, the Unión del Centro Democrático (UCD) went through a series of changes in its stance toward NATO. The memoirs of Rupérez reveal that by January 1981 Suárez had resolved to take Spain into NATO himself, but he was prevented from doing so by his early resignation.

As a consequence, the incoming government of Calvo Sotelo made the formal decision to enter NATO. Quite logically, given the circumstances, the decision was and continues to be hotly debated on several points. The first accusation was precipitousness. The decision was made with hardly any public airing of the question or debate within the Spanish political class. It is true that the growth of pro-NATO sentiment in the UCD could be observed in discussions at each successive party congress since 1978. In 1979, Rodríguez Sahagún, then minister of defense, favored Spain's entry into NATO, and Spain took a purely pro-Western stance in the 1980 Conference on European Security; the declarations of Adolfo Suárez became ever more explicitly favorable to NATO. A second criticism made by the Socialist opposition was that the government's move destroyed any political consensus on foreign policy. This complaint marked a distinction between socialists and centrists in 1982, but once the constituent convention was finished the need to maintain such a consensus was questionable. Without doubt, Calvo Sotelo's decision demonstrated personal bravery, especially in its initial moments, even though it was not followed by an aggressive campaign in the press or in the Cortes.

Fundamental to Calvo Sotelo's gambit was the irreversible character of a move like this one. Spain's entry into NATO did not further divide the UCD (a party fractured by internal tensions), as was demonstrated at the end of the debate when all of its members voted affirmatively. Neither did it necessarily constitute a Machiavellian maneuver designed to force the Partido Socialista Obrero Español (PSOE) to change its own position in the face of international pressures. The leaders of the UCD wanted to create a situation whereby the PSOE would come to its own realization, once in control of the government, that participation in NATO was in the national interest and was consistent with the transition from dictatorial to democratic rule. In the final analysis, the UCD was trying to put a PSOE soon to take power in the position of the

German Social Democrats, who opposed NATO until forming their own government and then made it the axis of their foreign policy. The foregoing were, in my opinion, the key factors in the decision that precipitated Spain's entry into NATO. Since that time, other factors that might have been involved, adding to or detracting from the wisdom of the decision, have been widely debated in the press. It has been said, in the first place, that it would have been possible to maintain bilateral relations with the United States as in 1953. But that would have meant merely performing a service to NATO rather than becoming a protagonist, and in the recent treaty negotiations with the United States the benefits of the multilateralization of the relationship were clearly felt. It has been alleged, secondly, that joining NATO amputated an arm of Spanish sovereignty. But Spain successfully defended the mandate for "denuclearization" which had been proposed and approved by Convergencia, so that it is reasonable to assert that Spain's entry into NATO actually enhanced its bargaining power internationally. Third, some argued that joining NATO was a response to the attempted coup or the result of other military pressure on the government. But the coup attempt really delayed the process of entry, which was always out of military hands altogether. The military was by this time sympathetic to NATO but offered opinions only when asked and showed no desire to participate in an essentially political decision. Fourth, there was some talk of a "French solution." But France's relationship to NATO is very different from what Spain's would be. Spain does not have the economic capability to maintain an independent deterrent force; nor would such an independent deterrent force have the same role in case of an attack through Germany; and Spain was not leaving NATO, as France was, but entering it for the first time. Finally, some have accused the government of ignoring Spain's own strategic interests in Gibraltar, Ceuta, and Melilla, and of having wasted a NATO trump card which might have been used in negotiating Spanish participation in the EC. But the strategic situation of Spanish interests in Gibraltar, Ceuta, and Melilla has not been altered in the slightest, and the supposed advantage of withholding Spanish participation in NATO in order to deal with the EC is nothing but speculation.

From first intimations of Spain's entry into NATO, the evolution of that process was indissolubly joined to the progress of Spanish politics. The anti-NATO campaign had allowed the PSOE to consolidate its popularity in the face of increasing divisiveness in the party of the government, doomed to watch its own support decline day by day. The language employed by Felipe González against the government (NATO, right off, no!) had a dose of ambiguity, but without a doubt it was interpreted unequivocally as a testimony of pacifism and reluctance to involve Spain in a militarist NATO. The propaganda of the PSOE was extremely effective in this regard. In 1975, 57 percent of the people surveyed in Spain had favored Spanish participation in NATO, but in 1983 that support had plummeted to 17 percent; those explicitly opposed had numbered 24 percent in 1975, but they had grown to 56 percent in 1983. The Socialist party had managed to erode the popularity of the government but did so by creating a climate of public opinion distinctly out of step with the rest of Western Europe. The current president of the Senate, José Federico de Carvajal, even held that a Soviet message of September 1981 suggesting that Spain not enter NATO was justified because of the position adopted by the government.

In October 1982, the PSOE took power with a program including a referendum on the subject of Spain's entry into NATO—a plan for which the PSOE had gathered hundreds of thousands of signatures during the previous Cortes—with Spanish military participation to be frozen pending the outcome. The new foreign minister, Fernando Morán, promised NATO members that Spain would remain faithful to the organization, but there must have been some ambiguity on the matter within his party. In 1983 Socialist leaders continued to make off-the-record comments hostile to NATO, and in the same year the vice-president announced his opposition officially with the backing of four ministers of the PSOE government. No real new developments occurred until October 1984 when González presented the Cortes a ten-point plan on Spanish defense policy.

In my opinion, the most intelligent defense of the transformation of the PSOE line concerning NATO has appeared in the writings of Angel Viñas. According to his thesis, the Socialist government has tried to elaborate a foreign policy at once autonomous, of the Left, and capable of its own initiatives, and to combine those objectives with a pragmatic approach to international affairs. In this fashion Socialist foreign policy could be said to contain enough realism to be viable and enough socialism to be a policy based on principle. In the case of NATO, Viñas argues that the PSOE position intended to link participation in NATO to other international forums like the Common Market, that it reduced outside pressures for a long period and so ensured for many years the autonomy of the Left of Spain's first government, and finally that a referendum provided for the kind of popular support for NATO present in all other participating countries.

Viñas' arguments are intelligent but really represent no more than an *a posteriori* rationalization. In truth, the Socialist leaders had many more reservations than one could infer from the formulation of implicit or explicit intentions offered by Viñas, whose thesis rather reminds one of Franco's descriptions of his own "skillful prudence" during the Second World War, during which he was in fact, by any objective measure, neither skillful nor prudent. The Socialist stance with respect to NATO can only be called skillful through rationalization of its essentially confused metamorphosis during the years before the referendum. The real imprudence of the PSOE policies may be judged by what happened next.

The greatest proof of this imprudence was the convocation of the referendum itself. It was the result of the Socialist president's confidence in his own popularity, and was carried out despite the fact that no one outside the government really wanted it and even though its final content was diametrically opposed to what the PSOE had originally proposed. Public opinion surveys up until the eve of the referendum continued to cast doubt on a positive result, which is unsurprising given the confusion of the proposition itself and the scant credibility of the arguments offered in its favor by the government. From my point of view, a vital question of international alignment ought to have involved an argument based on principle: the defense of liberty against a Soviet threat. But the proposition emphasized economic benefits and gains in military technology from participation in NATO, and its phrasing even gave the sensation of lack of commitment when it mentioned a reduction of U.S. military presence in Spain and showed a desire to avoid the military aspects of the alliance.

Nor was the political opposition especially lucid on this occasion. Some groups chose not to deal with the question at all. The opposition elements furthest to the Right committed the grave error of urging that people abstain from voting in the referendum. Had they opposed the referendum before its convocation this position would have been more reasonable, but adopting it afterward was rather indefensible from the viewpoint of their political counterparts in other European countries. A more coherent approach would have been to accept the right of voting in the referendum but to challenge the legitimacy of the results from the beginning. It is always hard to justify abstention, even from the most ill-advised election.

Whatever the political capital lost by the government and by the opposition, the worst consequence of all was the gratuitous damage done to the political system itself. The results of the referendum showed, first and foremost, the enormous disparity between the Cortes and the popular vote in a foreign policy matter of such gravity.

The result of the referendum has been received with satisfaction abroad, especially among those NATO members who, although they did promote Spanish participation early on, by 1986 viewed the Spanish decision with apprehension about what effect it might have in their own countries. Nevertheless, there are still problems associated with Spanish participation in NATO that are unlikely to be resolved in the short term.

Entry into NATO amounts to choosing a kind of society for Spain and a place for Spain in the world. Strategically, we have everything to gain, both at the global level and as regards particular Spanish national interests, including the modernization of the national armed forces. A distinction between civil and military participation is meaningless and can lead only to a loss of the active role that Spain today is capable of playing. NATO allows each member to tailor participation to its special situation. The function of Spain follows from its geographic position: a key role in defending the Strait of Gibraltar and the sea lanes of the North Atlantic. From this perspective, the restrictive policies of the current Socialist government are unnecessary and create a permanent tension with our allies. One wonders how much they really accept the Spanish position and how much they simply tolerate it for now. NATO is not a debating club but a military organization in which a refusal to participate in strategic planning makes little sense. Denuclearization may be an irrevocable decision of the Spanish people, but it demonstrates a certain lack of solidarity with the rest of the Western world and Spain can ill afford further displays of reluctance and restricted commitment. The good example is the current push for reduction of U.S. troops stationed in Spain. In sum, Spain's place in the defense of the West is not yet settled, nor have all the important problems in deciding that place disappeared. Because of the complexity of organization and command structures in NATO, and because of the simple fact that defensive strategy must be dynamic rather than static, Spain's position in the alliance must be better defined and must be expected to alter with time.

Then too, and this is the most important in my opinion, Spanish participation in NATO will continue to occupy an important place in Spanish politics, not because the decision to join is likely to be revoked, but because the absence of a broad consensus still make it controversial. The worst problem lies in a lack of identification with certain principles other Western Europeans hold in common. Spaniards do not yet perceive a Soviet menace, and until they do it will be hard to win general support for full participation in NATO. As a consequence, the behavior of the political class is somewhat schizophrenic in questions of national defense. Political parties always tend to strike different attitudes when in opposition and when in power. When in power they will have to be more realistic, while in opposition they will continue to exhibit a supposedly more autonomous and progressive (but frequently irresponsible) posture based primarily on the Spanish electorate's lack of information in foreign policy affairs. Two factors must be added to complete the panorama: first, the persistence of a certain anti-American sentiment in Spain (and not solely on the Left); and second, what has been called the "Almanzor Syndrome" (a feeling that the enemy is to the south rather than the east). The Almanzor Syndrome is nothing more than a demonstration of the uninformed and ingenuous nature of Spanish public opinion in strategic matters, since there is no danger to the south, and the behavior of our allies with respect to the problems of that region is not in doubt.

Bibliography

"España dentro de la Alianza Atlántica," seminar with the participation of Marquina, Oehling, Sáchez Gijón, Viñas, and others (Madrid: Instituto de Cuestiones Internacionales, 1986).

Hagemeyer, Bernard, Javier Rupérez, and Francisco Peña. España, *Europa, Occidente: una política de seguridad* (Madrid: Distribución y Comunicación, 1984).

Marquina Barrio, Antonio. *España en la política de seguridad occidental 1939-1986* (Madrid: Ediciones Ejército, 1986).

Rupérez, Javier. *España en la OTAN—Realto-parcial* (Barcelona: Plaza & Jánes, 1986).

2

Repercussions on the Democratic Process of Spain's Entry into NATO

Javier Pérez Royo

I am well aware that, as the *Equipo de Sociología Electoral* (Electoral Sociology Study Group) has written, "the influence of [the process of Spain's incorporation into NATO] on the consolidation of the representative and partisan institutions of Spain's young democracy will have to be evaluated when we have a greater historical perspective."[1] But I do not think it too soon to offer some speculations on the subject and examine them in the light of the initial steps of the process by which Spain became a part of NATO: the gradual configuration of the decision adopted by the government of Calvo Sotelo and subsequently ratified by the First Constitutional Legislature. Rather, I will focus on the final step of that process, the referendum through which the Spanish people ratified the decision of the Socialist government of Felipe González to keep Spain in NATO under specific conditions.

Undoubtedly, the initial phases of the process are interesting and without taking them into account it would not be possible to understand a good many later difficulties. The chief protagonists of these initial phases were well aware of the situation they were creating, as Calvo Sotelo himself once recognized:

> I suspected that the decision [to join NATO] would be particularly difficult for a government in which sectors of the left were certain to participate, possibly at high levels. . . . The decision to commit Spain to an Atlantic Alliance would not be easy for a government (or a coalition) of the left, though such a government might accept it as a *fait accompli*.[2]

For the purposes of this presentation, however, these are anecdotes without great importance. In spite of the bad faith in which they were executed, keeping the Socialist opposition completely in the dark "at a time when nobody had the slightest doubt about the imminent victory of the Partido Socialista Obrero Español (PSOE) in the upcoming general elections,"[3] and putting obstacles in the way of the future Socialist government, these final maneuvers of the government of Calvo Sotelo had scant effect on the workings of the Spanish democratic system.

On the other hand, the ratification of Spain's continued presence in NATO through the referendum of 13 March 1986 has had an important impact on our democratic system. Just how is a question that merits a more sustained examination.

The Nature of the "Consultation" and Its Consequences for the Political System

The relationship of *representative* to *direct* democracy has been among the thorniest matters that modern constitutional states have had to resolve in the practice of governance. Until now, excepting a handful of well-known but inimitable cases like that of Switzerland, stable representative institutions have appeared incompatible with frequent recourse to plebiscites and referendums. When these institutions of direct democracy have come into generalized use, the mechanisms of representative democracy themselves have suffered. For that reason, it is difficult today to find enthusiastic proponents of direct democracy at the national level. The commission named by the German Bundestag to study the possible reform of the Bonn constitution expressly rejected the idea,[4] and the case of Italy during the 1970s is well enough known in this regard.

Alerted, no doubt, by the Italian experience,[5] the Spanish constitutional convention opted for an extremely restrictive use of direct democratic institutions in general and of referendums in particular. This was one of the great topics of debate in the constitutional convention, where the generous use of direct democratic institutions at any cost was clearly a minority position, argued by the Alianza Popular (AP) alone. All the other parliamentary groups were quite hesitant to introduce institutions of direct democracy into the constitution, trusting that, even were they introduced, they would remain "unactivated" constitutional rights for a good many years.

Paradoxically, it would be a government of the Left that would take the decision to call a referendum in Spain, while the party that had defended a constitutional provision for referendums would oppose the call so strongly as to recommend abstention. The fear that referendums might become plebiscites, expressed by left-wing groups in the constitutional convention, was somehow assuaged. Meanwhile an inverse conversion was occurring among groups that had supported the inclusion of referendums during the constitutional convention. But let us move on to ask why the referendum was called at all, whether it served a useful function, and how it affected the general health of the Spanish political system. In sum, was it a good or a bad idea?

This question was insistently debated before and in the midst of the referendum campaign, during which the PSOE government itself long maintained a position of "calculated ambiguity" between the parties to the Left favoring a referendum, and the parties to the Right opposing it. Though formally in favor of calling a referendum, the government delayed setting a date.

The course of public debate on the referendum produced arguments in favor of all possible options, expressing the interests of each political group in the country, and it could not be otherwise. But the key question, the only one that can interest us more than two years after the referendum, is the following: Did the PSOE really want a referendum on Spain's participation in NATO, or did it intend to convoke a plebiscite on its own government?

That the referendum had many qualities of a plebiscite was undeniable. The justification given by the government for calling the referendum was that the PSOE had promised to do so as part of its campaign platform during the elections of 1982. This was true, but only half true, since the function of the referendum contemplated by the 1982 campaign platform was to *correct* some governmental decision rather than to *confirm* one. The way that things turned out, the referendum lost the character of a referendum and became, for all practical purposes, a general vote of confidence on the conduct of the Socialist government.

But was it no more than this, as the parties of the Right would have it, or was there more to it? Is it logical to believe that the government would convoke a referendum for that reason alone when, even if its programs should be ratified by the voters, the result was sure to limit the government's freedom of action in one of the most decisive aspects of its foreign policy? Isn't it more reasonable to think that the government had decided already what line it intended to follow in its foreign policy, and that it desired especially the direct backing of the electorate in order to overcome whatever political resistance might be marshaled by the opposition?

Obviously, this kind of reasoning will never be admitted on the part of the government, but it can be deduced from the declarations of politicians from other countries[6] and, above all, in the address of the chief of state in the *Pascua Militar* of that year, in which he expressly emphasized the need for "prudence" in negotiating the formula for Spanish participation in NATO "within the limits decided upon by the Spanish people." The reference is all the more significant because it was unnecessary and overobvious.

The government hoped the voters would "obligate it" to take the measures that it had itself chosen. In this way, a "loss" of freedom to maneuver became a positive aspect of the referendum for the government that called it and, at the same time, the formal character of a referendum was maintained despite the overtones of a plebiscite. Spain's current problems with the United States concerning the reduction of its military force in the country support this interpretation of the referendum. Could the Spanish government have as strong a position in the present situation without the vote of 1986? Would it be possible to try to force a solution without the commitment that the government is supposed to have derived in this matter directly from the voters?

Using a referendum in this way is unusual and not without its perils, but in my opinion this is indeed what was going on in the Spanish referendum of 1986. Now, given the preceding general outlines of the 1986 "consultation," the situation it has left in its wake is fraught with serious problems. I would emphasize two:

1. The very public opinion that is supposed to have determined the NATO decision tends in fact to be extremely skeptical about it. This was one of the great problems encountered by the Socialist party during the referendum itself, as the public opinion polls showed repeatedly. A majority of the Spanish people seemed convinced that the conditions debated for the referendum could never be made effective. And it would not appear that any of these reservations have diminished since then, at least as far as military integration and the removal of nuclear weapons are concerned.

2. But the most serious of the resulting problems for the functioning of our democratic system is the manner in which the government has attempted to compensate for its loss of liberty in foreign policy by taking greater liberties at home. Information previously available to the people at large is now concealed even from their elected representatives. The Official Secrets Law has been subject to an interpretation of dubious constitutionality in a recent resolution of the presidency of the Congress of Deputies, and it appears that the matter will soon be appealed before the Constitutional Tribunal.

How the tribunal will decide is difficult to predict at this time, though it seems certain that the case will be heard because the matter of constitutionality is so obviously in question. But whether or not the Constitutional Tribunal agrees that "the resolution of the president of the congress, ignoring the individual right [to information] of the representatives by restricting the free exercise [of that right], constitutes an infringement of Article 7 of the Congressional Regulations and of Article 10.2 of the Official Secrets Law, as well as of Article 20 of the Constitution," the mere existence of this kind of appeal says much, and little favorable, about the government's information policies and about its respect for the institutions of parliamentary democracy. The Official Secrets interpretation by the national executive and (less understandably) by the president of Congress, resulted "from a polemic arising when the government declined to inform congress about the content of a memorandum concerning NATO," and, continuing in the words of a newspaper that can hardly be accused of general hostility to the government, the interpretation provides "a light so restrictive or polarized that it effectively impedes the parliamentary function of control over important decisions of the executive."[7]

If the referendum was meant to give clarity and popular backing to Spain's entry into the Atlantic alliance, why so much mystery? Where is that clarity? If the political decision has already been taken and all that remains are technical formulas, why so many secrets? It would really seem to vindicate that skepticism and incredulity that so many voters expressed before the referendum and that the government is feeding now by its information policies, whether concerning the form of our integration into NATO or concerning the removal of nuclear weapons from Spanish soil. As *El País* wrote in its editorial "The Law of Silence" (January 29, 1987), "the second round of consultations or negotiations between Spain and the Atlantic alliance has ended for the public the way it began: in the most profound darkness. The official decision not to give information on this matter is patent. The secret cannot be excused with the argument that the negotiations are now in progress and one cannot tip his hand. The will to secrecy would rather seem dictated by particular political interests stemming from the government's promises to keep Spain out of the military structure of the Alliance."

By its nature, a question such as this does not usually lead to immediately threatening problems for the powers-that-be in a middling country like Spain with a well-established tradition of secrecy in military affairs. But at the middle and long ranges, repercussions like lack of credibility and mistrust toward the government are sure to surface, and the weaker the democratic tradition of the country, the greater those repercussions are sure to be. From this point of view, the consequences of the 1986 referendum have hardly been positive for Spain's political system.

Though the most obvious, this is not the only consequence the referendum on Spain's participation in NATO has had for our relatively new democratic system. There are, in my opinion, at least three more that ought to be mentioned.

A Notable Reenforcement of the Personalization of Power

This may be an increasingly general characteristic of contemporary European politics, but the case of Spain shows it in much higher relief than in the surrounding countries. Not even in other recently redemocratized countries like Portugal and Greece, not to mention the rest, has the weight of the individual leader acquired the importance that it has in the acquisition and maintenance of political power in Spain. Curiously, this phenomenon has intensified with the triumph of a Socialist party which, in principle, has always accented the collective elaboration of policies and decisionmaking by its governing bodies rather than by personalities which, however important, were supposed to remain in the background.

To the contrary, the PSOE has rested increasingly on the figure of the president, and reached perhaps the apogee of that tendency in the process of Spain's entry into NATO. If the initial policy of the party was defined collectively, none of the subsequent steps were. The chief executive presented himself to the Spanish people as the sole rectifier of that policy. He and only he determined the gradualist strategy through which information about the rectification was disseminated. He was the only negotiator inside or outside the country who dealt with the centers of power that had to be considered if the new strategy were to succeed. He provided the decisive, though not the only, support for the campaign that wooed the Spanish electorate into acceptance of an idea it had originally opposed. And finally, it was an exclusively personalist argument that proved conclusive in winning a majority acceptance of his formula for Spain's participation in NATO: Who would administer a negative outcome? To quote the Electoral Sociology Study Group:

> It is . . . probable that Weber would have recognized in González one of the charismatic leaders that the German sociologist defined

as characteristic of what he called "plebiscitary democracies," some features of which appear clearly in the referendum process.[8]

An Accentuation of the Crisis of the Right

The political crisis of the Spanish Right was probably inevitable and has deep underlying causes. Spain is one of very few European countries in which the construction of an urban industrial society was accomplished not only with virtually no participation of the Left in power (there are several quite significant European examples of this) but also in a complete absence of any counterweight for the Right because of the destruction of our democratic institutions. So it is logical that the Right's lack of democratic legitimacy should join with the historical necessity of making up for lost time and balancing our political system to produce the current crisis. Having grasped this at the right moment is, without doubt, one of the great merits of the current leaders of the PSOE.

This crisis has been accentuated by the policies of the PSOE, culminating with the referendum on Spain's participation in NATO. Even before that time, the Spanish Right had been having great difficulty formulating alternative policies to those instrumented by the Socialist government. Too often, it had taken refuge in a catastrophic diagnosis or prognosis that lacked verisimilitude and was rejected by the public. At the calling of the referendum the Right seemed to lose its sense of orientation altogether, and it became isolated from its "natural" supporters both inside and outside the country, as happened, for example, in the case of economic groups as important as the financial community (which issued a declaration favoring an affirmative vote), or in the case of the Church (which did the same, though rather more ambiguously), or finally in the case of important representatives of the international Right like Chancellor H. Kohl, the Bavarian politician Strauss, or Vice-President George Bush.

This situation in an election year could not but produce a negative impact on principal parties of the Right like the AP. A negative impact was already evident during the electoral campaign of June 1986, and from the day the results became public, that party's disintegration has accelerated. The result is a state of affairs, surprising for a representative democracy, in which the parliamentary opposition to the government is so based on coalitions (the *Grupo Mixto*) as to threaten the normal development of the legislature for lack of a real opposition at all.

Of course, this cannot be imputed totally to the effects of the referendum, but the referendum was clearly a decisive factor in accentuating the crisis of the Right and creating the situation in which we now find ourselves, with new voices, hardly suspect for alarmism or "catastrophism," daily denouncing the parliament's disconnectedness from reality.[9] This brings us directly to the third point that I would like to emphasize.

An Extrapolitical Channeling of Social Problems

From the moment when the PSOE took power, the combination of a large, absolute majority support for the government and an absence of credible political alternatives has led to a phenomenon rather infrequent in democratic systems: the channeling of social problems into a direct dialogue between the government and the affected sectors of society. Already occurring at various points in the previous legislature, the phenomenon has been exacerbated in the present legislature as a consequence of the increasing personalization of political power and the ongoing crisis of the Right. A few days ago, the cartoon editorializer "Máximo" expressed this aptly in a drawing of an embattled "Government" withdrawn to a fortress besieged by workers, businessmen, students, the *Grupo Mixto*, and we could add a long list of etceteras.

One cannot glibly assign political responsibility for this situation, which at any rate does not belong with the government since the "show" has been put on by all parties except the PSOE. But it is definitely another phenomenon strengthened by the form the referendum took and by the consequences it brought in train. In the immediate future of the current legislature, the dialogue channeled by our political institutions runs grave danger of not responding to what is happening in the country and even of having to be substituted by another kind of dialogue. Such a substitution indeed began to occur with the referendum, when practically all the parties (with the exception of a few super-minority groups like the PCE, EE, ERC) shifted away from their natural positions, and the tendency has since continued to grow.

By Way of Conclusion

The impact of the 1986 referendum on the general health of the Spanish political system cannot, I believe, be considered positive.

Aside from the tensions it generated (fortunately without dire consequences), and aside from the regrettable tone of the campaign and behavior of the major media, there has not been one real benefit resulting from its convocation. I do not think any social consensus was gained. The parties arguing for rejection of the proposition received only slightly more than one million votes in the past elections, but the cause they defended in the referendum received seven million. Despite near unanimity in the parliament in favor of joining NATO, almost 40 percent of the popular vote was against it. And we are supposing that the 53 percent who voted for the proposition were voting in favor of NATO and not in favor of Sr. González in order to avoid a power vacuum. Two years after the referendum, we can say with fair objectivity that it accentuated negative elements that were already present in our democratic system, elements that have not yet reached dangerous levels, but that we should begin to correct.

Notes

1. "El referendum del 12 de marzo sobre la permanencia de España en la OTAN y sus consecuencias sobre el sistema político," *Revista de Estudios Políticos*, 52, p. 212.

2. Cited by A. Viñas, Soberanía nacional y pactos militares, *Revista de Estudios Internacionales* 1 (1986), p. 17.

3. S. López de la Torre, "España y la OTAN," *Política Exterior* 1, p. 118.

4. R. Wahl, Emphelungen zür Verfassungsreform, AR (1978), Heft 1, p. 488.

5. A. Manzella, "El 7 de junio del año en curso el internacionalismo constitucional ha funcionado de manera fulminante," p. 330. "Il sistema parlamentare nel proietto constituzionale spagnolo," *Politica del Diritto*, IX: 3. (1978).

6. Manfred Woerner in *Política exterior*, p. 93.

7. *El País*, January 29, 1987.

8. *Revista de Estudios Políticos*, p. 212.

9. J. Sol Tura, *El País*, February 6, 1987.

3

Spanish Media and the Two NATO Campaigns

Inocencio Félix Arias

I shall begin by pointing out the obvious: The two NATO campaigns were extensively covered by the Spanish news media. The first of these campaigns was conducted by the Unión del Centro Democrático (UCD) government between August 1981 and June 1982, with a view to preparing for Spain's entry into NATO; the second took place under the Partido Socialista Obrero Español (PSOE) government in 1986, with the aim of keeping Spain within the alliance. I do not think that the term "campaign" is excessive, because both were carried out against the general current, with large sectors of public opinion showing a reticent or openly unfavorable attitude.

I shall distinguish, therefore, between the treatment accorded to the issue by the media during the initial stage or campaign for membership and the way it was approached when preparing for the referendum on staying in the alliance. First, however, I shall mention a feature that is common to both—the fact that attention was centered basically on the repercussions that the event might have in Spanish politics, on both the external and internal fronts. Practically all the media ignored the repercussions that the entry into NATO of a country of Spain's size and characteristics might have on the international scene.

The Campaign for Entry: Autumn 1981 to Spring 1982

Most of the media examined the issue in depth, thought about it seriously, and took up a particular stance. What would entry mean? Was it a good thing for Spain? Were they in favor? There was a wide variety of different positions. Leaving aside the openly hostile stances of *El Alcázar* and *Mundo Obrero*, opinions and positions ranged from wholehearted and unreserved support for entry on the part of *ABC, Ya, La Vanguardia* and *Cambio 16*, to the vague but unequivocally unfavorable view of *El País*, as well as other unsympathetic attitudes, such as that of *Interviú*.[1]

A good example of a clearly pro-Atlanticist stance is the series of editorials in the periodical *Cambio 16*, in autumn 1981, in which the beneficial effects of possible membership were outlined. These included:

1. Spain's isolation would come to an end.
2. Spain would be in a forum where freedom was defended.
3. The treaty with the United States was unequal. If there was to be an agreement with the United States, then it would be necessary to join NATO.
4. The armed forces would be modernized (editorial of September 9, 1981, entitled "In favour of joining NATO").

Several of these arguments were shared by *Ya, ABC, La Vanguardia*, and the now-defunct newspaper *Pueblo*.

Somewhat more subtle was the position taken up by the newspaper *Diario 16*, the offspring of the magazine *Cambio 16*, which seemed to be trying to convince its readers that membership of NATO was a minor but unavoidable evil. Was this due to disagreements among the editorial staff, or to concern about the pacifist tendencies of its readership? The fact is that, while supporting NATO, all kinds of attenuating explanations were offered: "We do not like NATO, just as we dislike any political option that involves a limitation on sovereignty" (editorial of January 3, 1982), or (in the same editorial) "The operation was carried out and, *apart from the trepidation and uncertainty to which this gives rise*, we should also point out that there are some positive aspects too."

Closer to the center of the spread of opinions were the magazine *Interviú* and *El Periódico*, published by the *ZETA* group. There was no editorial line, and in the large numbers of editorial writers, there were opinions of all kinds. However, those who claimed that entry would be beneficial were fewer in number than those who said it would be no help at all to Spain. This, together with the openly hostile attitude of the cartoonists, tipped the scales in favor of the anti-NATO option.

Further inclined towards an anti-Atlanticist position was the ever-formidable *El País*. The renowned daily never directly advocated an opinion opposed to Spain's entry, but it did express a number of messages that pointed clearly in that direction. The opposition of this newspaper both to entry itself and to the time it was being carried out, can be deduced from a number of observations.

1. An oft-repeated *editorial line* containing such categorical assertions as "membership will only serve to reduce our room for manouevre and ability to act on the international scene."
"All the NATO countries, with the exception of Portugal, Denmark and Norway, have got nuclear weapons. The constant promises not to bring nuclear weapons into Spain must be looked upon with suspicion."
"Our Atlanticist commitment is difficult to reconcile with our Latin American policy—one cannot serve two masters" (editorial May 18, 1982). There were other arguments of a more occasional nature: "With regard to the Falkland Islands, our imminent membership of NATO has deprived us of the possibility of adopting a position of our own."

2. A proliferation of negative-sounding news linked with statements and headlines (even on the front page) that are almost quaint: "Membership of NATO may prevent Soviet natural gas from reaching Spain" (November 6, 1981) or, paraphrasing in a sarcastic way a statement made by the then-minister of foreign affairs, "NATO will solve our foreign policy problems" (September 27, 1981), when the minister had merely said that it would help to solve some of them.[2]

3. Publication of a large number of cartoons clearly opposed to entry by the newspaper's cartoonist, Máximo, who had never concealed his opposition to membership (twenty-one cartoons in forty days). The captions systematically ridiculed the government's attempt to get Spain into NATO and its desire to throw overboard its "precious" neutrality.

The news media, apart from the essential issue, also paid a great deal of attention to the vicissitudes of the entry process itself. Considerable space was devoted to this, and special emphasis was laid on the obstacles, ranging from the suspense caused by rumors of Greek reservations over enlargement—"Expectancy over the attitude of Greece" (*El País* and *Ya*), "the signature was preceded by a secret declaration by Greece" (*El Periódico*), "Greece maintained its reservations until yesterday morning" (*Gaceta del Norte*)—to the campaign for the collection of signatures by the Socialist party aimed at forcing a referendum and holding up entry, a campaign regarded by many as merely a "symbolic gesture" (*ABC*), "an attitude by the PSOE to save face, one in which its organizers did not believe" (*Gaceta del Norte*), "a trick to save face" (*Ya*).

No less emphasis was placed by the media on the way in which entry took place and the depositing of the instrument of accession.

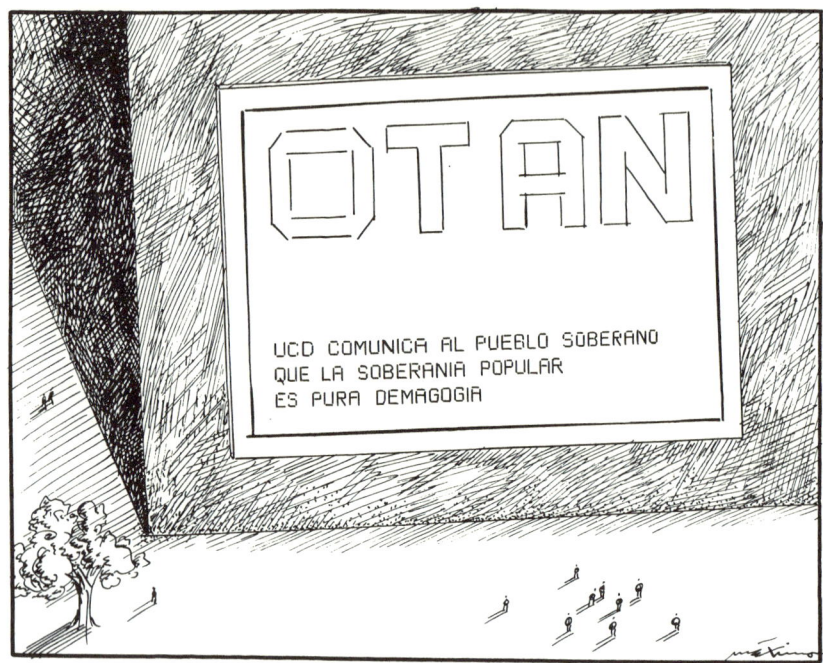

"NATO—UCD Informs the Sovereign People that Popular Sovereignty Is Pure Demagogy." (Cartoon by Máximo, reprinted by permission of the artist.)

Here, as *Diario 16* said on May 31, 1982, "UCD has completely lost the battle to present a credible image."

Diario 16 described the last stages as a "curious sprint to the finishing line," and *Tiempo* elaborated on this: "An almost clandestine ceremony in the State Department." Although the process of joining NATO was spread over nine months and parliamentary debates in both houses took place over the by-no-means-negligible period of nineteen days,[3] there was nevertheless an underlying impression in almost all the media (UCD had indeed lost the battle over its image) that the entire procedure had been rushed and some of its stages carried out in treacherous secrecy: "A tireless race to the Alliance in record time" (*El País*, May 18, 1982). The idea of overhastiness became so widespread (the decision to deposit the instrument of accession on a Monday which in America was a holiday was the last straw) that even *La Vanguardia* had to call it "our perhaps excessively hasty entry into NATO" (July 2, 1982), which was hardly reconcilable with its thesis, expounded on more than one occasion: "The centrist government, in accordance with its beliefs, carried out the process of joining NATO swiftly and without faltering."

"We Want More Guns, Butter Can Wait. Signed, The Brotherhood of Victims of NATO and the Warsaw Pact." (Cartoon by Máximo, reprinted by permission of the artist.)

The Attitude of the Most Pervasive Medium: Television.

As an autonomous corporation and a public body dependent on a government that was officially in support of entry into NATO, TVE (Spanish Television) tried to maintain a distant, neutral attitude by giving the pros and cons of the initiative. Nevertheless, it was often quite obvious that many of its producers had little enthusiasm for NATO. A key example of the scant sympathy for the organization was the most important program on the subject screened by TVE during this period. It was a long report devoted exclusively to the topic. The viewers were allowed to hear and see representatives of both options. No attempt was made to give priority to the supporters of the anti-NATO vote. However, the message was somewhat ambiguous as regards the "advantages" that might accrue to Spain. As a result perhaps of Third World, pacifist, and, in many cases, not particularly pro-American tendencies among its editorial staff, the fact is that TVE's special program did not add up to a particularly encouraging outlook. A somewhat overhasty view of the two blocs was given, and it was stressed that up to that time, Spain had not been involved in the possible dangers of belonging to one of those blocs. The repetition of war scenes and the display of weapons led viewers to the almost inescapable conclusion that membership in the organization would involve their country and themselves in a much greater risk than hitherto. The documentary ended with a summarizing sequence that must have confirmed this impression in more than one viewer: a veritable orgy of missiles, fires, explosions, and mushroom clouds descended on different geographical locations to the apocalyptic tones of the funereal *dies irae*.

The completion of the campaign—Spain's solemn entry into the organization—was described as a historic event by several of the media, such as *La Vanguardia, Ya,* and *ABC* (which in two editorials at the beginning of June 1982 reiterated a number of the advantages that had already been pointed out by *Cambio 16* in the editorial already mentioned). However, as a reflection of what we were saying at the beginning, that is, the concern about the effects of the event on domestic politics in Spain, the newspapers almost unanimously stressed that NATO could be an antidote to the temptation to organize coups. "A coup would paralyze our accession" said the headlines in *Ya* and *El Correo Catalán*; "Entry will stabilize democracy" said *ABC*, "Pérez Llorca tries to convince the allies of the definitive and irreversible character of our democracy" reported *El País, Cinco Días* and *El Noticiero Universal*. The emphasis was an accurate reflection of the concern felt by Spain at that time: the abortive coup at the hands of Tejero had happened only nine months previously and the media, like the citizens themselves, wanted to cling to a talisman. Consistent with its dislike for the aura of NATO, *El País* had previously declared: "The presence of the 'sick man of Europe,' Turkey, and previously that of Greece and Turkey, makes a nonsense of any identification of NATO with democracy."

The Winter Campaign: Referendum 1986

The referendum campaign was shorter, but also more intense and certainly more bitter than the one preparing for membership in the organization. It was almost unanimously agreed that there would be many who would suffer damage during the contest.

First, the government, and especially the president would suffer. On February 19 *Diario 16* said in an editorial entitled "González is his own victim": "The country now has in its hands the destiny of President González." *El Periódico*, the Barcelona newspaper, reiterated this idea on March 13 in an article entitled "Wear and tear on the President of the Government." *El País* supported the same thesis, saying that the outlook for the government during the campaign was gloomy and that the president would have to make an all-out effort, with all that this implied.

Nor did the opposition emerge unscathed. *El País* predicted that the position of Fraga and the leaders of the Right in favor of abstention would have consequences in the future. Subsequently, when Fraga resigned, some people were convinced that the issue and result of the referendum had helped to lower the morale of the leader of the Alianza Popular. Many of the media commented on the "discontent and puzzlement" felt by many Western conservative leaders at the attitude of their Spanish counterparts.

Even within the field of journalism itself there were skirmishes, clashes and casualties . This was the final link in the chain of events leading to the fall of the director of *Interviú*, P. Sebastián, an inveterate opponent of NATO, who had a further clash with the publishing firm, which was unhappy about his militant anti-NATOism. It was also the reason for the resignation of J. Pradera, the prestigious veteran editorial writer for *El País*. The editorial staffs of many newspapers lived through moments of confrontations and tension.

As regards the referendum itself, we must distinguish first of all different attitudes towards the very fact of calling it. There was a clear majority against the move (*ABC, La Vanguardia*), some of whom advised against it in virulent tones, while others did so in a subtler way. There was a second minority position that supported the holding of a referendum, represented notably by *El País* and a number of columnists from the *ZETA* group.

Once the holding of the referendum was accepted or condemned, the next stage was to examine the attitudes to the voting itself. Some media advocated abstention in an extreme manner. The chief representative of this position was the newspaper *ABC* and to a lesser extent the periodical *Epoca*. Some media did not come out with any opinion on the matter and others, such as *Diario 16* and *El País*, came down in favor of voting, the former having condemned the holding of the referendum and the latter having supported it. As regards the vote itself, of those supporting the vote a majority was in favor of an affirmative vote (*Diario 16, Cambio 16,* and *La Vanguardia*), and subliminally, the *SER* group and the magazine *Tiempo*. Others adopted a more ambiguous, less committed view, leaving all the options open, although at the very last minute, in a very vague manner, they seemed to hint somewhat obscurely that the consequences of a negative vote might be worse than those flowing from an affirmative one (*El País*).

Most of the media disapproved of calling the referendum. *ABC* was clearly against it, as was *Ya* ("The irresponsible referendum. The country is exposed to an unnecessary risk."); *Diario 16* said: "Those who have called the referendum will be called to account for this major political error when the time comes." Subliminally, the *SER* group also gave an opinion in this sense, for although it never actually took sides or expressed an opinion openly on the matter, having got rid of its editorial section, it did however disseminate the message that the holding of the referendum would be a mistake.

A slightly more subtle position was that of *El Periódico*, of Barcelona, which said in so many words that the holding of the referendum was morally the right thing but, at the same time, a political error.

Once the campaign got under way, certain members of the media began to move swiftly and decisively towards the idea of abstention. For example, *ABC* published a leader entitled "Ten reasons for not voting," in which it was argued that the question asked in the referendum was an electoral fraud and thus completely vitiated; a vote in favor would be a blank check for the government and therefore the best thing to do was not vote. The magazine *Epoca* seemed to suggest the same idea.

The morning paper *Ya* held an intermediate position. After coming out against the calling of the referendum and saying that the prime minister had worked "the miracle of making it impossible for anyone to vote in accordance with his convictions," the paper did not adopt a clear stance on abstention or voting one way or another. However, it seemed to be recommending participation, and called upon voters to think seriously about the significance of their vote: "Nothing will be the same again after this referendum."

A similar position to that of *Ya* was taken by the Barcelona newspaper *El Periódico* (editorial of March 9, 1986), which stated that there were moral reasons for voting for or against. It did not, however, express an opinion as to which was the most suitable, although it constantly stressed that the referendum should be binding. The Barcelona newspaper *La Vanguardia* went one step further. Having started by advising against the referendum (February 1, 1986) and then showing its irritation when it was called (March 6), it went on, with barely concealed annoyance, to call for an affirmative vote: "The consequences [economic, etc.] of a negative vote would be unforeseeable." "We must vote, and we must vote in favor, in order to break out of the impasse into which the government has thrust us."

Finally, let us examine the position of the influential daily *El*

"Scientific Belicosity; Utopian Pacifism." (Cartoon by Máximo, reprinted by permission of the artist.)

País, which had always been in favor of holding the referendum. It began by complaining about the question the voters were to be asked (editorial of February 1, 1986 entitled "The question of discord"), saying that it would be necessary to wait for the outcome of the parliamentary debate in order to express an opinion one way or another. When the time came for the newspaper to take a stand, it complained about the unwillingness of certain leaders to venture an opinion (editorial, "The leaders' silence"), but seemed itself reluctant to take up a position.

Finally, without recommending a vote either way (could there have been disagreement among the editorial staff?), it gave a vague impression of moving slightly towards the "yes" vote—although still in terms that precluded any possibility of its being "accused" of doing so—when it outlined the results of a negative vote: "Although we must not indulge in predictions of catastrophe," it might be assumed that "institutional tensions" could well arise.[4]

On the historic day of March 12, 1986, most of the media ran headlines indicating "suspense" and spoke of nervousness in government circles. The affirmative result was both categorical and surprising (52.55 percent in favor and 39.80 percent against).

"The day after," the general sensation was above all one of relief: "One of the most controversial and schizoid episodes of the infant Spanish democracy is now over" (*El País*). "The nightmare is over" (*La Vanguardia*). "We have finally resisted the attraction of the abyss. There was a great deal of Russian roulette in all this" (F. Onega in *Ya*). "The week of passion and calvary is over. There was something suicidal about this referendum" (J. Oneto in *Cambio 16*).

Attempts were made to explain how the miracle had happened. (Almost all the media had gone hopelessly wrong in their predictions and polls, which had expected a clear victory for the no's). What were the "reasons for the yes-vote," as the *Diario 16* headline expressed it (March 14, 1987)?

Perhaps the most commonly used explanation was that it was "the vote prompted by fear" (of economic and political destabilization) (*Diario 16* and *Cambio 16; El País* in "The hangover after the referendum," March 14, *El Periódico; ABC*).

Another reason offered was the effort made by the prime minister. *Diario 16* called it "a marathon personal campaign"; "He staked his all right up to the last minute," wrote J. Oneto in *Cambio 16*. "He has taken a beating" (*El Periódico*) and that of the government, which had used every means in its power (*El País*).

The maturity of the Spanish people was another possible explanation: "A sensible people" (editorial in *La Vanguardia*); "they'll send in their bill later" (*El País*); "the victory of the ayes is that of the nation as a whole" (*Diario 16*); "the Spanish people have bettered their rulers" (*Cinco días*).

A final reason given was the attitude of Spanish television, which was criticized and attacked from both Right and Left because of its "improper behavior in support of the vote in favor." In many people's opinion, this was noticeably different from the way it had behaved before, even during the early period of the Socialist government.

Spanish Television's (TVE's) coverage of the referendum campaign was indeed followed and judged with special attention by the other media. We may mention first of all a long report that was screened at the end of 1982 and the beginning of 1983. It gave an apparently neutral description of the organization, but at the same time it was clearly anti-NATO in tone. The "pacifist" and anti-bloc (= anti-NATO) atmosphere was palpable. The figure of the secretary general was ridiculed: "He has been accused of belonging to the Dutch Nazi party"; "in Spanish, he knows how to pronounce, 'Spain bullhide' [?]." And the negative aspects of NATO were exaggerated: "NATO looked on impassively while coups were taking place in

Greece and Turkey. NATO and at least the United States were implicated in the coup." The blocs were made to seem implicitly treacherous: "They have falsified relations between nations, distorting the political processes within." Special emphasis was laid on a long interview with an American former admiral who deployed all the anti-NATO arguments that might have an effect on Spanish public opinion: Once you are in NATO, it is useless to try and prevent the entry of nuclear weapons, the standard of living of the Spanish people will decline, the First and Second World Wars were fought in Europe and the Third will be too, and so on.

The behavior of Spanish Television during the winter campaign was unanimously felt to be different. *Diario 16* and *Cambio 16* headlines declared: "As a result of the manipulation by Spanish Television, which it has not even taken the trouble to try and conceal on this occasion," damage has been done to the very essence of a public communications medium. *El País* stated: "It [TVE] has followed the official line in a stifling manner, and has not served society as a whole." *ABC* claimed that the people who interviewed the prime minister were much less aggressive with him than they were with his rivals and referred to "TVE's imprisonment of the government's opponents." "TVE: never again," declared an editorial *Ya*, on March 15, which concluded with the words, "our society simply doesn't deserve this sort of thing."

Negative Polls: a Godsend

I should like to end by discussing the opinion polls published in the news media. These polls were a total failure. With the exception of an *Epoca* poll, all of them were hopelessly wrong. We may take the following percentages as a sample:

	No	Yes
El País	52–56	40–46
La Vanguardia	35.5	24.8
Diario 16	51	45
SER (Sermómetro)	12.715	7.435
(Chances of either result)		
Epoca	43	49
Actual result	39.79	52.55

I wanted to emphasize this because I am convinced that just as much as the prime minister's efforts to persuade the electorate, or the possible influence of television or any other reason, it was the opinion polls, with their constant and apparently inescapable negative forecasts, that brought about a crucial change in the outcome of the vote. The insistent way in which the press kept repeating that the no's would win prompted an unspecifiable number of Spaniards who had not intended to vote to do so and to vote in favor of NATO. I am convinced that the constantly repeated publication of the negative polls in the media was a decisive influence in helping the government win the referendum. Or to say this another way: if it had not been for the polls, the no's would have won.

Notes

1. Circulation figures of newspapers and periodicals are:

		Period
ABC	218,739	1985
Diario 16	130,461	1985
El País	348,364	1985
El Periódico	136,947	1985
La Vanguardia	191,123	1985
Cambio 16	151,860	1985
Epoca	106,267	1985
Interviu	284,865	1985
Tiempo	136,304	1985
TVE	7,500,000	1985
SER	3,209,000	1986

2. Backed by Calvo Sotelo, the minister, Pérez Llorca, was the person who really carried the burden of the campaign from the government side and consequently was the target of the attacks of the anti-NATO group.

3. Two weeks in committees in the Congress and Senate, and almost two weeks in plenary sessions in both houses.

4. From quite different angles, *Mundo Obrero* and *El Alcázar* asked bluntly to vote "no."

4

Spain, A Singular Ally

Joaquín Abril Martorell

I shall attempt to illuminate the sometimes ill-defined contours of Spanish public opinion concerning our country's entry into NATO and its subsequent role in that organization. The series of peculiarities characteristic of Spain, the paradoxes and ambiguities of the international context, and the particular paths followed among the alternatives offered by recent history together explain the title of "Spain, A Singular Ally."

Spain has been the last country to join NATO, with many years separating its entry from those that preceded it. This is not merely a historical accident, but the result of a clearly separate historical experience. My intention is to sketch only the broad outlines of a phenomenon of indubitable political significance: the tangle of ambivalences and ambiguities among which Spanish perceptions concerning NATO necessarily move.

Such ambivalences and ambiguities also color our relationship with the United States. It is worthwhile to stop and consider the far-reaching consequences of this fact. If Spain has a political sin, the sin is ingenuousness. Our sentiments regarding NATO do not flow from clear, shared calculations, but from thwarted general principles and unilinear logic. Spain does not have its back to modernity, but stands perplexed before it.

Let us proceed to develop this thesis first by discussing several historical singularities of Spain in relation to other countries of Western Europe, then by pointing out several errors that NATO itself has committed, and finally by revealing certain basic ambiguities in Spanish perceptions of NATO. These ambiguities, as we shall see, arise at the confluence of Spanish historical singularities and the organization's errors.

Spain: A Singular History

The North Atlantic Treaty Organization has roots deep in the history of Europe. The presence of the United States in the alliance is the result of that country's decisive intervention in the European theater of the Second World War.

In the aftermath of the Second World War, the centuries-long struggle for supremacy in Europe seemed to have been resolved finally in favor of Russia—now the Soviet Union. European supremacy appeared a first step to world domination. A conviction that such were Soviet intentions, the growing strength of communism as an alternative ideology, and the unequivocal loss of world hegemony by England and France combined to inspire the creation of NATO. The present members joined the alliance successively and each for its own reasons.

But the shared historical experience that has enabled the vigorous maintenance of this alliance over a long period of time has not been Spain's historical experience. Spain's historical experience presents important divergences from the Western European pattern. We will mention here only those that bear directly on participation in NATO.

1. The Spanish state retains a clear memory of having been what today would be called a "superpower." The center of European history—which would be from that moment the center of world history—came to rest in Spain and Portugal at the close of the fifteenth century. Spain, upon whose domains the sun never set, retained hegemony over all of Europe for a century and a half, and remained a major power for another century and a half afterward. But if Spain is well aware of having been powerful, it is equally aware that the axis of history no longer passes through Spanish meridians.

2. Spain has not lived with a Slav or Moscovite threat as have the Germanic peoples and the Turks. Russia is not a historical enemy of Spain.

3. Spain has not had the interaction with Russia that England, France, and Germany have had during the last two centuries. Russia has simply not been present in the Spanish consciousness.

4. Spain has not been a historic competitor among the peoples of northern Europe, in contrast with England and France who struggled for European supremacy during an entire century. Historically, the Spanish people have had a good image of Germany.

5. Nor did Spain experience German occupation during the Second World War, unlike all of the rest of continental Europe. Spain

has not had the historical experiences that led to a special treaty with regard to Germany.

6. The intense experience of the Spanish civil war, with its antecedents and sequels, served to attenuate some of the differences already mentioned, but it did not always push Spanish sensibilities in the direction of those of the majority of Europeans. The sequels, at any rate, permitted the inculcation of a widespread fear of communism, which eventually brought Spain into the cold war and to its first treaty with the United States, parallel with the creation of NATO.

7. For three decades Spain was not fully accepted as part of the West, so that the loss of China, the Korean War, and the other major events of the cold war that turned the North Atlantic Treaty into a permanent military organization were not viewed at the time as matters of direct national interest in Spain. Unlike the initial members of NATO, Spain had no part in defining the responsibilities, commands, and territories, or in equipping and promoting the organization.

8. Nor has Spain participated in the important steps taken subsequently by NATO, like the partial pullout from France or changes in strategic doctrine such as that of "double decision." Therefore, the Spanish people have only a limited idea of the security implications of changes that take place within NATO.

9. During the thirty years between 1945 and 1975, the Spanish people were fed an elementary anticommunism focused on the Soviet Union. The consequence was an alignment with the West based on an oversimple reaction.

10. Spain did not experience directly the reconstruction of Europe, the process of decolonization, the emergence of the Third World, the movement toward détente, or other constitutive elements of the contemporary international scene, all of which remained in the distant background of Spanish national life.

NATO: Errors

A long, shared European historical experience has constituted the cement for a treaty organization the cohesiveness and durability of which can only be explained as a coincidence of national interests among the member nations. These disparate national interests have come together in a common interest: to conjure a Russian menace that, for the member nations, is real, believable, continuous, almost palpable.

In defense of that common interest, the treaty's permanent military organization has suffered vicissitudes and adopted successive forms. Such transformations can be explained by the diversity of national power, economic weight, and political trajectory among the countries that make up the alliance.

The structure of NATO is not strictly functional; it does not represent an optimization of defense imperatives. Judged purely from a military point of view, NATO's structure is unnecessarily heterogeneous, highly asymmetrical, and, taken together, rather irrational.

The current European situation in terms of economic potential and a political stability is quite different from that which existed when the feebleness and ideological divisions of a war-devastated Western Europe necessitated a Marshall Plan, a North Atlantic Treaty, and finally the creation of a permanent military organization.

The original impulse toward European unity has been diluted and the strategic doctrine has been reoriented by technological advances, both phenomena accompanying a continued dependence on the United States. As a result, if one forgets history and examines the structure of NATO from the perspective of military efficiency, a number of incongruities are evident.

In fact, NATO's structure, its deployment, and its overall strategy are no more than reflections of the political and economic factors that conditioned its creation. Even admitting the (essentially nineteenth-century) conceptions with which the alliance was forged, one finds a series of paradoxes that result finally in the errors to which we refer. The following are a few examples.

1. NATO is an organization in which the United States plays a decisive role. Nevertheless, Germany, France, and Great Britain together could probably defend themselves against the Soviet Union. The difficulties lie in the fact that Germany, France, and Great Britain are very different countries with perfectly individualized armed forces and foreign policies, and in the fact that Germany lost the Second World War.

The absence of European unity and the peace terms imposed on Germany make the American ally indispensable. At heart, they are two aspects of the same phenomenon. Germany is simultaneously an ally and a defeated enemy, a complication that makes a united European armed force as yet unthinkable. For that reason it has often been said that the problem of Europe is Germany.

NATO was formed to defend Europe, but only under conditions that keep Europe from being able to defend itself, despite its industrial and demographic capacity to do so. As a defensive alliance, NATO is distorted by imperatives prior and even superior to its defensive purposes.

2. The organization of NATO is asymmetrical. The United States contributes the nuclear weapons and retains the ultimate decision as to their use in European territory. France and England have their own nuclear forces not assigned to NATO, and, at least in principle, they have the autonomy to decide their use. Germany has been prohibited from making nuclear arms but has to provide the nuclear battlefield. The remaining countries neither have nor will have nuclear weapons.

Summarized in this way, the strategic needs of these three European countries are contradictory. Germany most requires frontline defense, but it lacks the capacity for nuclear deterrence. France and England possess a nuclear deterrent but do not require frontline defense.

The United States, by manning the front line in Germany, solves the problem of protecting that country from the Soviet Union's presumed aggressive intentions, but at the cost of further distortions in the structure of the alliance. Not only does Western Europe require an American ally to defend it, but it requires that ally on the front line.

These are all consequences of root problems already described: the lack of real European unity and the continuing question of Germany. The permanence of this state of affairs makes of NATO mostly another modality of the confrontation between the United States and the Soviet Union.

3. Let us now look at a third level of complications. The U.S. troops are on the front line partly to make clear that an attack from the East would be, both symbolically and in fact, an attack on the American ally. According to often-repeated declarations, this could rapidly escalate into a nuclear engagement.

In this way, the asymmetries within NATO are responsible for the forced nuclearization of European defense strategy in the hands of the non-European member of the alliance. Though defense and nuclear war are no longer conceptually dissociable, the implications of such a situation are unacceptable. A nuclear war would be the last war, and it must be avoided at all cost.

4. Europe has been brought to this state of affairs by a chain of decisions, situations, and events, almost all of them protagonized by the United States, in which Europe has been involved hardly at all. To mention a few: (*a*) the use of atomic bombs against Japan in the Second World War; (*b*) exclusivity in the availability of nuclear weapons after the war; (*c*) the subsequent struggle for nuclear

superiority; (*d*) the prohibition on German possession of nuclear weapons; (*e*) the doctrines of nuclear parity and mutual assured destruction; (*f*) the strategy of flexible response.

Without entering into details, it is enough to say that the United States' own political, economic, and military concerns, along with its responsibility as a world power, have oriented the strategy and deployment of U.S. forces in Europe. And the concrete military threat that hangs over Europe has likewise taken shape in virtue of the complex global contest between the United States and the Soviet Union.

Spain and NATO: Ambiguities

What has been sketched out thus far allows us to see: (1) how the creation and durability of the North Atlantic Treaty were responses to diverse and complex causes, with roots deep in a European historical experience which Spain does not share; and (2) how the military organization has continued to respond to technological advances and to the moves of the communist adversary, another complex process in which Spain has not taken part.

Under the circumstances, it is hardly odd that Spanish public opinion, in contrast with public opinion in the leading NATO countries, has paid little attention to the strategic game, its moves, or the stakes involved. The natural result has been a series of ambiguities felt by the Spanish people regarding the whole process of the alliance, ambiguities that cannot be cleared up by government decisions, nor by pacts among elites, nor even, it may be, by the critical examination of issues that simply do not have the density of direct experience for Spaniards. Rationalization is no substitute for experience of this kind, and a long time will be necessary for that experience to begin to accumulate.

Consequently, and regardless of the validity of the decision that was actually taken regarding Spain's entry into NATO, the ambiguities are there and will remain for some time. Let us briefly consider some of them.

1. The best way to understand NATO is as a manifestation of the general confrontation between the United States and the Soviet Union. Doubtless, the particulars of the European context are important, since they have decisively affected the strategic doctrines of both superpowers, but the overriding logic is nevertheless that of global confrontation.

In this confrontation the United States and the Soviet Union share the rationale of mutual assured destruction and display congruent strategic doctrines and patterns of military deployment. The present situation has grown out of the two world wars and the following pattern of European disunion, neither of which processes involved Spain at all.

Now, the perception which has been popularized within Spain is that of a NATO founded for defense of Europe, in which all Western Europe has joined and in which Spain, too, ought to join in the spirit of European solidarity. Possibly the factors enumerated in the section "Spain: A Singular History" do not permit any other approach in promoting the idea.

But the simplification of a question so profound and complex betrays itself in an important ambiguity. The fact is, as the origins and subsequent career of the organization reveal, that NATO keenly demonstrates the incompleteness of European unity, contradicting the rationalization of a unanimous, resolute Western Europe with a solid front to aggression. The myth whereby Spanish backwardness results from not assimilating with the rest of Western Europe is invoked again to buttress these vulnerable rationalizations of European solidarity.

2. The supreme evil of political demonology, at least in the Spanish version, is nuclear armament. The nuclear arsenal's thousandfold multiplication of previously existing destructive power has been thoroughly publicized for years, and it has been newly reinforced by a popularization of studies on the possibility of a "nuclear winter."

Until now, the only nations with the practical capacity to eradicate human life have been the United States and the Soviet Union, and they have acquired that capacity as a result of successive actions or decisions with which other nations have had little or nothing to do. Under the doctrine of flexible response, the United States has declared its intention to use that capacity when it considers necessary, so that by joining NATO Spain enters into this most extreme form of military confrontation. It should be pointed out that the denuclearization of Spanish territory does not alter this situation in the least.

The result is an ambiguity between Spain's will to denuclearize and its entry into a military alliance organized explicitly around the capacity and intention to use nuclear arms under certain conditions, with no guarantees whether or how Spain could remain outside such a nuclear engagement were it to occur.

3. The threat of nuclear war between the two superpowers brings

with it another consequence, rather unexpected in the light of what has been said so far. It is increasingly suggested that a unilateral ban on nuclear armament in Europe would not be sustainable, in the middle run, in the face of a Soviet nuclear arsenal. There is a growing perception that the credibility of a U.S. nuclear umbrella could not be indefinitely maintained, so that Europe would drift into an irrevocable "Finlandization" as a result.

In the light of these perceptions a third ambiguity emerges. What has been presented in Spain as the supreme evil, the evil of nuclear weapons, is viewed by Spain's European neighbors as a lesser evil. And this goes beyond paradox.

4. The discontinuous and uneven progress of Spain's entry into NATO has impeded a prior accord concerning the specifics of Spanish participation. For example, it is not clear what Spanish responsibilities will be with regard to maritime space, especially in the Strait of Gibraltar, much less with regard to Gibraltar itself. The real value of Spain to NATO has not been fully discussed either. Is it simply as a base, or as a greater territorial depth? Will it make a genuinely military contribution?

Perhaps the principal value of Spanish participation in NATO consists in its symbolic effect, signaling unequivocally the position of Spain in the confrontation between the Western and Eastern blocs. For the signal itself to be stabilizing, it is not necessary for Spanish military forces to make a significant contribution. Thus the real importance of Spain to NATO itself constitutes another ambiguity.

5. If NATO is above all an expression of confrontation between the superpowers, it is not the only expression of that confrontation. Therefore NATO is not the United States' only interest in Spain. The renewal of the bilateral treaty between the two countries presents another problem, one that has passed unnoticed until now, one that contains within itself yet another ambiguity. The treaty between the United States and Spain is either redundant with respect to NATO or completely incomprehensible.

Considerations

One

To this point, the present argument might be accused of historical determinism, but such a criticism would be unfair. There do exist certain determinants in history whose impact delimits what is possible and makes the historical process to some degree predictable.

Let us mention some examples of such determinants in the

aftermath of the Second World War: the defeat of Germany and its consequent incapacitation as a dominant world power; the abandonment of imperial pretensions by England and France; the replacement of German domination in Central Europe and the Balkans by Slavic domination there; Western Europe's capacity for industrial recuperation; the will to power of the Soviet Union; and the impossibility of the United States' resigning its role in the international order.

Nevertheless, the march of history retained a wide latitude of development within the limits set by this configuration of factors. We will discuss only two examples of that latitude.

First, Western Europe might have responded to the Soviet challenge by uniting in a supranational state rather than by continuing in a system of sovereign nation states. After some vacillation it elected the second alternative. At that point the entrance of the United States into the strategic game became necessary, as it would not have been in the case of the first alternative.

A second area of indeterminacy was the successive elaboration of doctrines of foreign policy, the situations analyses for a multitude of different countries, the reckonings of military power, the evaluations of future trends, and the formulations of strategies, of budget choices, and of technological alternatives. Any of these could have gone differently from the way they actually did in either the United States or the Soviet Union. There was nothing obligatory in the sequence: Hiroshima, Strategic Air Command, Sputnik, Cuban Missile Crisis, M.A.D., arms talks, Flexible Response. In a word, the outcome of Soviet-American relations after 1945 might have been very different.

The present observations have merely surveyed events that did occur and that interacted with a people's historical experience to form perceptions of the present. It has been shown that, given the European bifurcation initially adopted, people's perceptions depend essentially on the reactive relationship between the superpowers, with all the errors and paradoxes that it entails. As for the place of Spain within this context, no further comments are necessary.

Two

It would not do to omit mention, however brief, of a second consideration. The contingencies to be contemplated in a hypothetical conflict are quite varied:

- A war between NATO and the Warsaw Pact, or a war of superpowers.

- A war on the central front, or on NATO's southern flank; deep fighting on the central front, or a fixed line of engagement.
- Conventional war, a tactical nuclear exchange, or a strategic nuclear exchange.
- A war in Europe, or in the weak underbelly of Southwest Asia.
- A war between blocs, or between individual powers. A direct war, or a war by proxies.
- An open war, or a local conflict.

Obviously, if we go on to consider patterns of technological development at the middle and long ranges, the strategic logic changes, becomes speculative, and may well be incompatible with present approaches. Therefore strategy, equipment, and deployment are in a permanent state of evolution.

For this reason, the inclusion in NATO of a new member country and the negotiation of a new treaty with the United States are problematic affairs, still more in the case of a country whose geostrategic position is as singular and as significant as Spain's. While the United States must attend simultaneously a whole gamut of global strategies in flux, Spain must attend pressing particular needs of its own—threats to political stability, a referendum, modernization, and so on.

Three

It has been impossible, for lack of time, to qualify these remarks with considerations of proposals of zero or double zero disarmament options.

Four

It is often said that the advent of nuclear power opened a new historical era. This is surely true, but it would be more exact to say that the power of the atom combined with high-speed delivery systems to create the new age.

Only thirty minutes would be sufficient to make the planet Earth uninhabitable for human beings. And perhaps ten minutes (just six hundred seconds) would be enough if the destructive power presently available were concentrated in submarines. This is a consequence of the physical constants of the old laws of Newton. Let us turn our attention for a moment to other physical limits.

Given the scant minutes within which an enemy attack must be detected and countered, radar and other means of detection must distinguish between a possible attack and all other physical phenomena (including unidentified ones) that similarly affect the detection devices. Another physical limit comes into play here: the physical capacity of detection and discernment in the devices being used. This physical capacity can never be absolute, but must always be relative to the length of the wave, relative to some finite dimension.

Precisely because of the demands of attempting such fine discernment, our computational abilities threaten to exceed another physical limit, this one much more difficult to measure—the limit of computation without error. The simple possibility of computer error, and of other kinds of error, requires that human intervention be present in the unleashing of whatever nuclear response results from the logic of confrontation between the superpowers. And the time available for human intervention to judge the probability that an attack is real and to assess the possibility of some kind of error is only a few minutes in the case of ICBMs, and almost no time at all in the case of SLBMs. We are in the presence of a war humanly impossible to control. Physics puts limits on what man can do with technology. The limits of rationality and of human control are of transcendental importance on two levels.

First, these limits illuminate the untenable and incompatible relationships of the various levels in the logic of confrontation between the superpowers, making clear why such relationships must be simplified as much as possible. For example, a Spain aligned with NATO and facilitating its logistics in the Mediterranean would simplify a number of levels of strategic logic for the United States.

There is another level more subtle but perhaps more important. Linear thought, the domination of nature, the limitless advance of empiricism, and the fundamental myth of scientism finally reach their own limit, a blank wall reminiscent of the perceptions that derive from the ideological irreducibility of the antagonistic blocs.

There are questions that are not soluble "rationally." I chose not to place this final, radical ambiguity among the others of the foregoing discussion, but it is there among them nevertheless.

In Conclusion

In sum, we have reviewed some of the historical singularities of the country that has been induced to join NATO thirty years after its formation. Because the historical experience of Spain did not impel it to take that step, it was necessary to invoke other reasons. The most persuasive of these was the desire to show solidarity with a Europe, more specifically with a European Community, which has only lately accepted Spain as a member. But we have seen, too, how idiosyncratic is European solidarity from the point of view of defense.

For an American executive, it must be difficult to coordinate the peculiarities and special desires of small nations of Europe within the planetary dimensions of superpower strategies. But for the European countries it is likewise difficult to understand the maze of complementary and surrogate logic subordinate to the principal logic of a war which, more than singular, seems humanly impossible, and if it were possible, less than human.

Spain may well be a rather singular ally, but NATO itself is rather singular as well. And well beyond the bounds of singularity is the concept of a final war for which NATO is preparing itself.

PART 2
SPANISH FOREIGN POLICY, THE UNITED STATES, AND THE WESTERN ALLIANCE

5
Atlanticism and Europeanism: NATO and Trends in Spanish Foreign Policy

Emilio A. Rodríguez

On March 12, 1986, Spanish voters went to the polls to vote in a national referendum on whether the country should remain in the North Atlantic Treaty Organization or modify its participation in the Atlantic alliance. The referendum, which received little attention in the public media in the United States, was of great significance to both the NATO alliance and the domestic politics of Spain. (See the Appendix at the end of this chapter.) As late as ten days before the vote, opinion polls indicated between 52 and 56 percent of those voting would cast "no" ballots against the government's position.[1] The results of the vote were surprising. Of those voting, 52.3 percent voted "yes," 39.84 percent voted "no," and 1.09 percent cast blank ballots.[2]

Never before had a NATO member taken the issue of participation in the organization to its voters. A rejection of continued membership in NATO would have presented a strategic problem for the alliance since Spain represents an important geographic base for resupplying forces in Western Europe and controlling the Strait of Gibraltar in the event of a conventional confrontation with the Soviets in West Germany and France.[3] Furthermore, given popular tensions throughout Western Europe over the deployment of the Pershing and cruise missiles, a rejection of NATO by the Spaniards, if followed by government withdrawal from the organization, could have set a precedent sparking demands for similar referenda throughout the alliance, especially in Greece. Spain, the newest member of NATO (1982), could have seriously damaged the integrity of the Atlantic defense system.

In domestic politics, the political future of President Felipe González and the ruling Partido Socialista Obrero Español (PSOE) hung in the balance. The Socialists, who had swept into power in the October elections of 1982, had proclaimed the referendum as an important plank in their political platform.[4] While never officially promising withdrawal, a majority of the leadership during the 1982 electoral campaign, including Vice President Alfonso Guerra and Foreign Minister Fernando Morán (1982-1985), did support a foreign policy of strict neutrality which would not permit Spain to be associated with NATO.[5] The shift toward favoring permanence in NATO by the González administration led to some fragmentation within the PSOE coalition. Simultaneously, the conservative Alianza Popular (AP), led by Manuel Fraga, attempted to maximize the NATO issue to gain political support, questioning the goals of the Socialist government and the validity of the referendum itself. In the end, the ability of González to maintain party discipline and to convince the electorate of the government's new position, resulted in both the maintenance of Spain in NATO and a resounding political victory for the PSOE, culminating in the parliamentary elections of June 1986.

This paper will focus on the NATO referendum and its broader impact on Spanish foreign policy. In January 1986, Spain and Portugal formally entered the European Community (EC). In March, Spain reaffirmed its commitment to defend the Community of Twelve. The results of the referendum must also be interpreted as popular confirmation of the official government policy of European integration. The vacillation between a strong commitment to strategic and economic integration in Western Europe and the *tercermundismo* (identifying Spanish solidarity with the Third World) policies of the early democratic period in Spain has been resolved. Spain has fully cast its lot in with Western Europe. This "European orientation" will have subsequent effects on Spain's international relations with both the United States and Latin America. These two regions constitute an Atlanticist option for Spanish foreign policy, which has been an historically important alternative for policymakers dating back to the Franco regime.

Atlanticism, Europeanism, and the Peculiarity of NATO

The review of Spanish foreign policy from the Franco regime to the contemporary democratic socialist period demonstrates a dialectic between Europeanism and Atlanticism. This tension was born in 1939 with the crisis of legitimacy and search for international recognition by the governments of General Francisco Franco. By Europeanism, we refer to the commitment to a fuller participation (economic and political) in Europe and the European integration process symbolized by the EC. The alternative to this foreign policy focus is Atlanticism, which focuses on developing closer economic, political, and military ties with two distinct regions: the United States and Latin America. Generally, the literature refers to Atlanticism as the nearly exclusive domain of U.S.-European relations. That is to say that Atlanticism is restricted to an analysis of North Atlantic relations. Here, we are purposefully broadening that interpretation to include Latin America. This region must be considered in the discussion of Atlantic options for Spain, as several Spanish governments have made Latin America an important component of their foreign policy strategies.

Spanish international relations with the Western Hemisphere can be easily distinguished between the special strategic relationship between Spain and the United States on the one hand, and the unique historical and cultural ties with Latin America on the other. The important trend that emerges, beginning with the Franco regime, is: During periods of economic and political difficulty with Western Europe, Spanish decisionmakers will emphasize and maximize ties with the United States and Latin America. Conversely, during periods of economic and political cooperation with Western Europe, foreign policy decisionmakers tend to ignore Latin America, and seek to limit strategic relations with the United States.[6]

In the Spanish chess match of foreign policy, NATO is a curious institution. Though dominated by the United States and not formally or institutionally connected to the EC, this multilateral military organization has nonetheless obtained an important role in the calculation of Spanish foreign policy. On the one hand, NATO is generally analyzed as an Atlantic strategic relationship that integrates American and European military resources and planning. In the case of Spain, however, membership in the multilateral organization has more recently been used as a tool to maximize integration into Europe with the specific goal of reducing the bilateral military relationship that Spain has had with the United States since 1953.

As shall be further examined in a later discussion, during the first government of the PSOE (1982-1986, including the Cabinet reshuffle of 1985) NATO membership clearly, though unofficially, became tied to Spanish entry into the EC. At times, maintenance of NATO membership was used as a carrot by Spain's European neighbors responsible for voting Spanish entry into the EC. On the other hand, the González government would utilize the spectre of possible Spanish withdrawal from NATO as a stick, during the negotiation for

Spanish entry, whenever Community members seemed to be delaying Spanish membership in the EC.

In the second, and current, PSOE government (1986-present), the multilateral relationship with the United States in NATO is being used as a bargaining chip in order to reduce the bilateral, and direct, U.S. military presence in Spain. Specifically, President González, his defense minister, Narciso Serra, and his foreign minister, Francisco Fernández Ordóñez, have been pressing for the removal of U.S. F-16s from the Torrejón air base outside Madrid and refueling tanker planes from the air base at Zaragoza. Concession by the United States to this Spanish demand would effectively mean the removal of the United States Air Force 401st Tactical Wing from Spanish territory.[7]

The Integration of Spain into NATO

The arguments that swirled around the question, by 1986, of whether Spain should remain in NATO cannot be separated from two related issues: the United States-Spain military base agreements of 1953 and the manner by which the Unión del Centro Democrático (UCD) government of Leopoldo Calvo-Sotelo entered Spain into the alliance. The leadership of the PSOE, which in the 1970s was adamantly opposed to both the U.S. bases in Spain as well as Spanish entry into NATO, would later try to use continued participation in NATO in return for a reduced American military presence in Spain as a carrot before the electorate.

The primary foreign policy goal of the authoritarian regime of General Francisco Franco in the post-World War II period was international recognition.[8] On December 2, 1946, the General Assembly of the United Nations had voted, in Resolution 39, to exclude Spain from all organizations associated with the United Nations. Furthermore, the Resolution recommended that all ambassadors be withdrawn from Madrid. Spain was to be punished for its close ties to the Axis powers during World War II. Only Portugal, Argentina, and the Dominican Republic, all dictatorships at the time, maintained their ambassadors in Madrid, along with the representative of the Holy See. When the United Nations lifted its recommended diplomatic sanctions in late 1950, the ambassador of the United States presented his credentials in Madrid in February 1951.[9] With the outbreak of the Korean conflict, and the cold war, the United States determined that Spain could play an important strategic role in the defense of the Mediterranean.

Though the Truman administration could not convince NATO members to accept Spain into the alliance, it did begin negotiations with Franco which ultimately integrated Spain into the strategic plans of the United States to encircle the Soviet Union with a defensive belt of Western bases. The Madrid Pact was signed in September 1953 between the United States and Spain. Defined as an Executive Agreement, the pact did not have to be brought before the United States Senate for approval as a treaty. It contained three agreements: a defense agreement, an economic assistance agreement, and a mutual defense agreement.[10]

The defense agreement allowed the United States to establish three Strategic Air Command (SAC) bases (Torrejón, Zaragoza, and Morón) and one naval faciltity (at Rota), as well as a series of other military communications facilities throughout Spain.

The economic assistance agreement was critical to Franco. Though it tied U.S. assistance to monetary and financial stabilization in Spain, it prepared the groundwork for Franco's Stabilization Program of 1959.

The mutual defense agreement was qualified by U.S. commitments by treaty to its other European allies. Thus the United States maintained the right to interpret the conditions under which the agreement could be invoked.[11]

The military agreement with the United States was negotiated at a critical time for the Franco regime. Spain had endured heavy physical suffering in the post-civil war period. International diplomatic ostracism, since the late 1940s, and the emergence of a maquis underground resistance movement in the Pyrenees, had raised hopes in the political opposition dominated by the Communists and Socialists that the regime was teetering. The U.S. base agreements seemed to have salvaged the Franco regime from collapsing on its own by providing important recognition status and economic resources to the regime. The agreements were followed in 1955 by the United Nations lifting Resolution 39, thus reintegrating Spain into the international system. From 1953 until 1986, the Spanish Left would not forgive the United States for salvaging the Franco regime in the name of anticommunism. The position of both the PSOE and the PCE (Partido Comunista Español) would be to press for increased limits on the U.S. military presence in Spain.

The bilateral treaties of 1953 were significant because they drew Spain directly into the American-led system of European defense, but did not integrate Spain into the multilateral command structure of NATO. The Spanish military strongly desired integration into NATO. When the bilateral agreements came up for renewal in 1963,

1968-1970, and 1976, the United States used the carrot of eventual Spanish membership in NATO during negotiations. Nonetheless, the European allies in NATO remained firm on barring Spain from membership so long as Franco remained at the Spanish helm.

The death of Franco, on November 20, 1975, was not accompanied by any fundamental changes in the foreign policy of the first government of the monarchy of King Juan Carlos I led by Carlos Arias Navarro. The foreign policy objectives of the government during this period were to:

1. improve relations with bordering countries: Portugal, Morocco, France, and Great Britain (because of Gibraltar);
2. renegotiate and renew the bilateral base agreement with the United States, which was due for renewal in 1976;
3. establish contact with the nations that made up the EC and NATO;
4. improve relations with the Roman Catholic Church; and
5. send a message to the Latin American countries explaining the significance of Spain's entry into the orbit of democratic nation states.[12]

The primary concern of Spanish foreign policy in the immediate post-Franco period was renewed focus on simultaneously improving European and Atlantic relations. However, this globalist strategy did not achieve its expected goals. The search for integration into Western Europe did not lead to any concrete diplomatic advances during the Arias government. The international expectation of rapid and dramatic change in the domestic political process and structure in Spain was not met during the tenure of the Arias government. Despite Foreign Minister Areilza's claims that Spain was entering the "democratic orbit," the Spanish system had remained fundamentally unchanged: the franquista political structure maintained control, with the participation limited to players of the old regime. Spanish foreign policy sought to legitimize a new regime that had not yet been established.

The transition to democracy in Spain began in earnest with the appointment of Adolfo Suárez to the presidency of the government in July 1976, and includes the goverments of the UCD of Suárez (1977-1981) and Leopoldo Calvo Sotelo (1981/82). The "transition regime" introduced the structural and institutional changes necessary for the establishment of democracy in Spain. The diplomatic style of the government changed dramatically. Whereas Arias had little interest in foreign policy, Adolfo Suárez sought to incorporate it as a fundamental part of his political strategy. The president dominated the foreign policy sector with his "executive diplomacy," exemplified by many trips throughout the world, but especially to Latin America.[13]

Under Suárez, the foreign policy of the transition period seemed confused. One of the chief criticisms was that the president should have concentrated more on relations with Western Europe, especially with social democratic countries, such as West Germany and Britain, with which he would have had a natural political affinity. The preoccupation with *tercermundismo* was seen as an attempt to vividly demonstrate that Spain was assuming a "new" role in the international system, and to try and capitalize on instant prestige in Latin America.[14] The result was that Spanish integration into NATO became a secondary issue, while in the area of integration into the EC, negotiations proceeded, but at a rather slow pace. It would seem that Adolfo Suárez attempted to use the policy of *tercermundismo* in order to appear more Left of Center than his political past would suggest. With the legalization and participation of the Communist and Socialist parties in the new democracy, Suárez tried to evolve into a populist political alternative, a strategy which led to fragmentation in the UCD and the president's ultimate resignation in 1981. The UCD made Spanish entry into NATO part of its electoral platform in 1979.[15]

President Leopoldo Calvo Sotelo, who replaced Suárez in February 1981, represented the more conservative sector of the UCD. Furthermore, he was an avowed supporter of Atlanticism as the focal point of Spanish foreign policy. With his foreign minister, Pérez Llorca, Calvo Sotelo introduced NATO membership for parliamentary debate on October 27, 1981. The timing of entry was critical, as 1981 was also the year in which the military base agreement with the United States came up for renewal. The UCD government saw the year as a critical one for determining the future course of Spanish security policy within Europe. As the foreign minister at the time noted, "Spain, since 1953 had been *de facto*. though not formally, in NATO, and should [in 1981] formalize its position in the Alliance, now that that is possible, or move into a position of clear neutrality. The real options are for Spain to become a part of NATO and insert the bilateral relationship [with the U.S.] within that context, or go to a clear situation of neutrality which would break complete defensive ties with the United States."[16]

Throughout the debate, the two sides on the issue reflected the ideological positions of the parties on strategic policy. The PSOE and the PCE adamantly opposed entry into NATO. Their position was "neither NATO, nor the bases." The PSOE, under the leadership of Felipe González, demanded that the issue be placed before the electorate as a referendum. On the other side, the ruling UCD coalition and the conservative Alianza Popular, supported entry.

On October 28, 1981 the Congress of Deputies approved Spanish application for entry into NATO by a vote of 185 in favor, 146 opposed.[17] On November 26, 1981, the Senate similarly approved entry by a vote of 106 in favor and 60 opposed.[18] What followed was a massive mobilization by the PSOE to rally support for its anti-NATO campaign.

On November 10, 1981, the Atlantic Council of NATO began the process of ratification, by which each member state of the alliance would have to ratify Spanish membership. This part of the process would last until May 1982. The issue, however, had not been completely settled, and the outbreak of the Malvinas/Falklands War between Argentina and Great Britain in April 1982, produced new strains within Spain which inevitably reopened the debate on the proper balance between a European and a Latin American commitment by Spain in its foreign policy.

Although the government had succeeded in getting the Cortes to approve Spanish membership in the Atlantic alliance during a time in which public opinion also favored membership, the political future of the UCD was dimming. The first formal notification of the decline of the party arrived on May 25, 1982, when the UCD lost in the Andalucian regional elections to the PSOE. In October 1982, national elections were to be held. More importantly, the government believed that the PSOE had begun mustering enough support in the Cortes to reopen the debate on NATO in the legislature.[19]

When word arrived that the Greek government had ratified Spanish NATO membership (the last country to do so), President Calvo Sotelo instructed the ambassador of Spain in Washington to deposit the approved NATO membership documents on Sunday, May 30, 1982, thus making Spain a formal member of the Atlantic alliance. As noted previously, the government feared that on Monday, the PSOE could have prevented NATO entry in the legislature. The PSOE would rally around this unorthodox method of "Sunday entry," to further mobilize public opinion against the UCD and its political methods. The complaint against imposed membership became one of several planks in the PSOE electoral platform for the October elections of 1982. It should be noted that although the UCD government was able to obtain Spanish membership in NATO and did join the political bodies of the organization, it nonetheless announced a freeze in full military integration. This was partially due to the increasing inability of the party to exercise political leadership at the national level, and the growing fragmentation and splintering within the party itself.

The PSOE, NATO, and Foreign Policy: 1982/83

The foreign policy the Socialists sought to implement following their overwhelming victory at the polls was intended to introduce an alternative *via* from the *tercermundismo* of Adolfo Suárez and the North Atlanticism of Calvo Sotelo. Promoting a general approach of abstention from the international East-West polarization, the basic goals of the first PSOE government were to:

1. negotiate Spanish entry into the European Community;
2. hold a referendum on Spain's permanence in NATO, a corollary of which would be to seek the reduction of the U.S. military presence in Spain;
3. improve relations with Spain's European neighbors, particularly France, Great Britain (Gibraltar), and Portugal;
4. improve relations in the Magreb, with special reference to the security and future of Ceuta and Melilla; and
5. promote political and economic ties with Latin America with an emphasis on a Spanish role to support democratization throughout the region and to seek a negotiated peace in Central America.[20]

Support for the first goal, acquiring the entry of Spain into the European Community, reflected a strong national consensus which cut across ideological and political lines. Given the economic crisis that the country was facing (and has yet to resolve), membership in the EC was a must for the long term economic health of the Spanish economy. Furthermore, in the eyes of the Socialists, integration into Europe would signify the conclusion of the franquista era once and forever. The EC represented political as well as economic acceptance by Europe, thereby demonstrating continental confidence in the consolidation of Spain's democracy.

Foreign Minister Morán and many other groups within the Socialist coalition believed that membership in the European Community could be pursued independently of the strategic question about permanence in NATO.[21] Article 99 of the Socialist platform for the 1982 elections promised to freeze further military integration into NATO, and reaffirmed the Socialist promise to convoke a national referendum in which the public would determine the future of Spain's membership.[22] Simultaneously, Article 83 promised to make the national defense more independent and sovereign, while articles 94 and 95 promised to support peace, disarmament and détente as well as the nonnuclearization of Spanish territory. Together these positions reflected what was in 1982 a fairly strong consensus within the PSOE that Spain should unlink itself from the U.S. strategic bloc in Western Europe.

During the first year of government, the González cabinet would seek to alter its North Atlantic ties with the United States. Nonetheless, there was an important political resource to be developed in the South Atlantic and Caribbean: Iberoamerican relations. While an entire volume could be written on relations between Spain and Latin America, it is sufficient to note that given the cultural and historic ties, not only between Spain and the region, but specifically between the PSOE and Latin American political parties through the Socialist International, the government believed that it could successfully project its international image in the region.[23] Somewhat reminiscent of the earlier executive diplomatic style of Adolfo Suárez, in 1983 and early 1984, Felipe González made several triumphant trips to Latin America, the most notable of which were the inaugurations of Raúl Alfonsín in Argentina and Jaime Lusinchi in Venezuela. Simultaneously, the PSOE government further widened the gap between Madrid and Washington by both recognizing the legitimacy of the Sandinista junta in Nicaragua and offering political support to a negotiated settlement in Central America.

The End of PSOE Consensus on Foreign Policy: 1984–1986

By 1984, divisions began to emerge within the PSOE government and party on the direction of Spanish strategic policy. First, there was continuity in the desire to limit the bilateral strategic relationship with the United States. However, on the issue of permanence and further integration of Spain into NATO, in both the government and the party there was a lack of consensus. Foreign Minister Morán continued to favor close ties with the Third World while totally opposing integration into NATO. The vice-president, Alfonso Guerra, voiced similar views on NATO, which resulted in a policy debate in the cabinet following his anti-NATO declarations in an interview with *El País*.[24] President González did not support the Guerra position which called for complete withdrawal from NATO.[25] Cabinet ministers Javier Solana (culture), José María Maravall (education), and Ernest Lluch (sanitation), openly support the Guerra thesis.[26] The head of the Instituto de Cooperación Iberoamericana (ICI) and PSOE activist Luis Yáñez, not only questioned the permanence in NATO, but at times even questioned the benefits of entry into the EC. The Yáñez position was reflective of Spanish frustration in 1984 with the lack of movement on the part of the European Community to finalize negotiations on Spanish entry. The President of ICI proposed deepening Spanish ties with Latin America as a possible alternative to the EC.

To the "right" of these positions stood President González, Defense Minister Serra, and Economics Minister Miguel Boyer. The president remained strongly committed to the following positions:

1. Spanish entry into the EC;
2. holding the promised referendum on NATO; and
3. reduction of the U.S. military presence in Spain.

González differed with the left wing of his cabinet, and by 1984 openly supported permanence in NATO as a means of achieving Spain's entry into the EC and the reduction of U.S. forces. The shift to a pro-NATO stance by the chief executive was the result of a linkage established by the Europeans, tying entry into the EC to permanence in NATO and the belief of González that the adoption of a French model of participation in NATO would be the best strategy for reducing the direct U.S. presence in Spain.[27] The EC and NATO are independent institutions and therefore the Europeans never explicitly, or formally, made Spanish integration in the Community contingent on permanence in NATO. Nonetheless, during state visits by the president the discussion of the two multilateral organizations was closely linked. Appearing on French television in May 1984, González, when asked about the government's position on NATO, reiterated that "Spain could not turn its back on assuming its share of the responsibility for the defense of the West."[28] The President's preference for maintaining an option of continued presence in NATO was further expressed during the debate in the Congress of Deputies on the state of the nation, October 24, 1984, during which time González presented his "decálogo" (ten points on Spanish foreign policy).[29]

Tensions in the cabinet, exacerbated by problems in the domestic as well as international sectors, led in July 1985 to the first reshuffling of the Socialist government since it had assumed power in 1982. The initial push for change revolved around the removal of

Foreign Minister Morán and Economics Minister Miguel Boyer. Differences over the NATO issue and the lack of movement on EC entry were seemingly linked, as demonstrated by the European response to their removal.[30] The appointment of Francisco Fernández Ordóñez to head the Foreign Ministry was greeted with satisfaction by NATO representatives who welcomed the "definite end of Spanish governmental ambiguity with respect to NATO."[31]

On November 9, 1985, Felipe González declared that the entry of Spain into the EC was directly tied to the permanence of Spain in the Atlantic alliance.[32] Furthermore, he stated full personal support for maintaining Spanish participation in NATO as it currently stood. A month later, in an impressive political move at the party congress, González was able to maintain party discipline to support the position of his government despite the fact that Socialist public opinion opposed NATO membership. The result was the publication of a document, "Paz y seguridad en España," which was approved by the Executive Federal Committee of the PSOE. The move by the government to support permanence in NATO was reinforced by a vote in the Congress of Deputies on December 27, in which an absolute majority of legislators voted to support the government's pro-NATO stance.

Moving fairly quickly, in spite of popular demonstrations by the far Left (Partido Comunista Español and disobedient sectors of the Socialist coalition) and an official policy of abstention from participation in the referendum by the Coalición Popular, the government put the question before the voters on March 12, 1986. The resulting victory of 52.5 percent of the electorate voting to maintain Spain in NATO was achieved following a massive television campaign by the president, who exploited his personal popularity with the voters to win the greatest test the PSOE faced since gaining power in 1982.

Atlanticism and Europeanism Revisited: Postreferendum Spanish Foreign Policy

In retrospect it would appear that the conclusion of negotiations for Spanish entry into the EC was facilitated by the reshuffle of the cabinet in July of 1985. The removal of a chief antagonist to keeping Spain in NATO, Fernando Morán, and his replacement by a pro-Atlantic alliance foreign minister revived European confidence in Spain's commitment to the multilateral defense of Europe. Following the referendum, the NATO ministers accepted a Spanish document defining the mode of Spanish integration into the alliance.[33] Spain will contribute to the collective defense, but will remain outside the military structure. Participation in political councils within the organization will be continued.

Entry into the EC and the multilateralization of defense indicate that the PSOE Government, which successfully gained another five-year term of office after the June 1986 legislative elections, has opted for full European integration.

The tension between Atlanticism and Europeanism has been partially resolved. The major tension resulting from the decision to seek security through multilateralism has revolved around the future of U.S. military bases in Spain. The bilateral Spain-U.S. treaties expire in December 1988. The Spanish government has made their renewal contingent on the reduction of the U.S. Air Force presence at Torrejón and Zaragoza. This would leave U.S. forces at Morón and at the submarine base at Rota.

The U.S. argument is that the removal of the seventy-nine F-16s from Torrejón would constitute a serious weakness in the defense of southern Europe, which could not be assumed by the Spanish Air Force alone. The Spanish response was that such a reduction has been adequately compensated for with the decision to remain in NATO.[34] While members of the Spanish far Left did not get their wish of "ni OTAN, ni bases," neither will the United States get its preferred outcome of "both NATO and bases." The tactic of Felipe González to use the Europeanization of Spain's strategic defense in order to reduce what was perceived to be a potentially damaging bilateral North Atlantic military relationship may yet be the single most important outcome of the March referendum. Closely linked to permanence in NATO, and a topic we have not been able to consider in this paper, is the issue of Gibraltar. Negotiations on the future of the Rock continue between Great Britain and Spain. The Spanish government maintains that it is inconceivable that Spain and Great Britain be members of both NATO and the European Community, and Britain still occupy a territory to which Spain lays claim.

With regard to Spanish foreign policy toward the South Atlantic and Caribbean, much of the early optimism exuded in both the government of Adolfo Suárez and the first PSOE government has worn off. The economic constraints under which Spain operates as a middle power facing its own economic crisis, have reduced the outlook for significant development of new economic ties between Spain and Latin America. Nonetheless, the PSOE government maintains the Spanish tradition of identifying Spain as a natural bridge between Latin America and Europe. In fact, European actors such as West Germany have been developing close ties with Latin America independent of Spain. In spite of this, the Spanish government has utilized its new integration into Europe as a means of focusing European attention on Latin America, especially on the Central American situation. Participation in San José III, the third meeting between representatives of the EC and nations involved in the Contadora process, has served to reinforce the Spanish position on Central America. This is another area of contention between Spain and the United States, the latter of which would prefer to reduce European attention given to Central America.

At times the analogy of "the two Spains" is too freely applied in the analysis of Spanish politics. To approach the historic tensions between Atlanticism and Europeanism in Spanish foreign policy using that analogy would be to oversimplify an ongoing interaction of diverse and conflicting national interests. Spanish ties with Europe, the United States, and Latin America are part of a broader zero-sum game as the analogy of the two Spains might imply. The tension between Atlanticism and Europeanism will remain in Spanish foreign policy. That foreign policy will continue to adapt to continuously changing environmental and political factors. Further research on this area must consider the role and policy position of moderate and conservative political parties in Spain who, in strategic themes, are the strongest supporters of close strategic ties with the United States. Between now and 1990, when new elections must be held, the foreign policy of the PSOE government has been defined: (1) maximize the economic integration into Europe as a support for alleviating a deteriorating domestic economy; (2) maintain participation in NATO while supporting increased multilateral decisionmaking within the organization (so as to reduce American domination of NATO decisionmaking); (3) renegotiate the bilateral military accords with the United States with a view to reducing the direct presence of the American military in Spain; and (4) in Latin America, continue to support democratization and maintain an independent foreign policy vis-à-vis Central America that can emphasize the opportunities for nonmilitary solutions in that region.

In pursuing its Atlantic and European goals, Spanish foreign policy will probably continue to generate tensions with the United States, who must become accustomed to the fact that Spain will no longer be as quiescent an international actor as it was under the Franco regime. In fact, the increasing multilateralization of Spain's economic and strategic ties in Europe should enhance Spanish sovereignty and independence of action in both Europe and the

Western Hemisphere. In the short run, Felipe González, the pragmatic Socialist, may yet achieve more of his international objectives than domestic economic stability despite the great turbulence during the national debate on Spain's foreign policy in the 1982-1986 period.

Notes

1. *El País* (Edición Internacional), March 10, 1986, p. 11.
2. *El País* (Edición Internacional), March 17, 1986, p. 1.
3. For a discussion of the strategic importance of Spain in the Mediterranean region, see among others: Tomás Mestre Vives, "El papel de España en la estrategia meditérranea," in *Historia* 16, October 1980; Antonio Sánchez-Gijón, *España en la OTAN* (Madrid: Ediciones Defensa, 1978); and Gen. Eduardo Munilla Gómez, "La seguridad europea y las fuerzas armadas españolas," in Sociedad de Estudios Internacionales (SEI), *Jornadas informativas sobre temas internacionales* (Madrid: SEI, 1985).
4. See Equipo de Documentación Política, *Un año para la esperanza* (Madrid: PSOE, 1983).
5. See Fernando Morán, *Una política exterior para España* (Barcelona: Editorial Planeta, 1980).
6. See Howard J. Wiarda, ed., *The Iberian-Latin American Connection: Implications for U.S. Foreign Policy* (Boulder Colo.: Westview Press, 1986).
7. *El País* (Edición Internacional), March 23, 1987. Significantly, however, Spain is not asking for a complete U.S. military withdrawal from its territory. The current Spanish bargaining position would maintain the U.S. naval facility at Rota.
8. The single best publication on the foreign policy of the Franco era is José Mario Armero, *La política exterior de Franco* (Barcelona: Editorial Planeta, 1978).
9. Armero, p. 158.
10. See Esther Barbé, *España y la OTAN* (Barcelona: Editorial Laia, 1984), pp. 57-61. Note also that in 1984 the Spanish government began declassifying documents from 1953, which should provide further research on U.S.-Spanish relations during this period.
11. See Antonio Marquina, "El sistema defensivo de España durante el franquismo: 'las bases'," in *Historia*, October 1980, pp. 36-47.
12. Sergio Vilar, *Proyección internacional de España* (Madrid: Editorial Tecnos, 1981), chap. 2, "Conversaciones con José M. de Areilza."
13. For an examination of Spanish foreign policy toward Latin America during the transition, see Eusebio Mujal-León, "Iberoamérica en la nueva política exterior de España," or Emilio Rodríguez, "Transición a la democracia en España: ¿Hacia una nueva política iberoamericana?," both in Instituto de Cooperación Iberoamericana, *Realidades y posibilidades de las relaciones entre España y América en los ochenta* (Madrid: Ediciones Cultura Hispánica, 1986).
14. See Vilar, chap. 3, "Conversaciones con José Mario Armero." Armero accuses Suárez of embarking on a leftist foreign policy (à la Willy Brandt) without taking into account that he himself was a product of the reformed

Right. Therefore, Armero argues, Suárez visited Cuba but could not "communicate" with Fidel Castro.

15. See José Pedro Pérez Llorca, "De cómo y por qué entramos en la Alianza Atlántica," *Ideas para la democracia* (Madrid) 1984, p. 13.

16. Pérez Llorca, p. 314.

17. *El País*, October 29, 1981, p. 1.

18. *El País*, November 27, 1981, p. 1.

19. *El País*, October 29, 1983.

20. For a discussion of the foreign policy of the PSOE, see: Angel Viñas, "La política exterior y de seguridad del gobierno socialista español," in Instituto de Cooperación Iberoamericana, *Realidades y posibilidades de las relaciones entre España y América en los ochenta* (Madrid: Editiones Cultura Hispánica, 1986); and the formal position of the PSOE as expressed in its document, "Paz y seguridad en España," approved in December 1985 by the Comisión Ejecutiva Federal del PSOE.

21. Among those in the PSOE coalition opposing any form of membership by Spain in NATO were Izquierda Socialista, Juventudes Socialistas, and sectors of the Unión General de Trabajadores.

22. See "Cien medidas por el cambio," reprinted in *Un año para la esperanza*, published by the Equipo de Documentación Política (EDP) of the PSOE (Madrid: EDP, 1983), pp. 90, 99.

23. See Tomás Mestre Vives, "La política iberoamericana del gobierno socialista español," monograph 27, Instituto de Cuestiones Internacionales, March 1985; or, Luisa Treviño, "La política exterior del gobierno socialista hacia Latinoamérica," in *Revista de Estudios Internacionales* 6, no. 1 (January-March 1985).

24. *El País*, July 17, 1983.

25. President González did not publicly differ with his vice-president. However, following a meeting with Alianza Popular leader Manuel Fraga, Fraga emerged from the meeting stating that González did not support the full withdrawal of Spain from NATO. The president never denied this statement by the opposition. In fact, the president's silence on his personal stance on NATO was notable until the pronouncement of the "decálogo" in 1984. *El País*, July 19, 1983.

26. *El País*, July 20, 1983.

27. This linkage was openly stated by Lord Carrington, secretary general of NATO, even after Spain entered the European Community. *El País* (Edición Internacional), January 6, 1986.

28. *ABC*, May 7, 1984.

29. *El País*, October 25, 1984.

30. It should be noted that Spain formally entered the European Community on June 12, 1985, a month before the cabinet reshuffle. Nonetheless, several NATO representatives seemed pleased with Morán's demise.

31. *El País* (Edición Internacional), July 8, 1985.

32. *El País* (Edición Internacional), November 11, 1985.

34. *El País* (Edición Internacional), March 23, 1987.

APPENDIX

The NATO Referendum in Spain, March 12, 1986:
The Question and Conditionality Clauses

The Government considers it in the national interest that Spain remain in the Atlantic Alliance and resolves that established on the following terms:

1. The participation of Spain in the Atlantic Alliance will not include its incorporation in the integrated military structure.
2. The prohibition on the installation, storing or introducing nuclear arms on Spanish territory will be continued.
3. The progressive reduction of the military presence of the United States in Spain will be proceeded with.

"Do you consider it advisable for Spain to remain in the Atlantic Alliance according to the terms set forth by the Government of the nation?"

Source: Revista de Estudios Internacionales 7, no. 1 (January–March 1986).

6
European Community Enlargement and the Evolution of French-Spanish Cooperation, 1977-1987

Glen D. Macdonald

Relations between France and Spain have improved dramatically in recent years. This is an extraordinary development in view of their troubled relationship since the early nineteenth century and, not surprisingly, the road to French-Spanish cooperation has been as rocky as the Pyrenees that separate the two countries. To understand the present state of relations between France and Spain, it might be useful to examine why and how they succeeded in overcoming obstacles in the path toward rapprochement. This should also permit some commentary on future trends in their relationship. With these objectives in mind, I will examine the evolution of cooperation between Paris and Madrid during the past decade.

The history of European affairs might lead one to conclude that the major obstacle to French-Spanish cooperation when Franco died in 1975 remained the differences inherent in voisinage, or neighborly proximity. Subsequent events indicate, however, that while sharing borders has often exacerbated the strains in their relationship, the heart of the problem between France and Spain was profound divergence in worldviews and national interests. That would change and so too would the nature of the relationship. Indeed, there has been a remarkable convergence of French and Spanish interests since Spain became a democratic state, joined the European Community (EC) and elected to remain a NATO member. During the past decade, France and Spain have resolved their differences on Basque terrorism, negotiated away the obstacles to the Community's enlargement, diffused the fishing imbroglio in the Bay of Biscay, and laid the groundwork for further collaboration by establishing institutionalized channels of communications between their ministers and heads of state. This transformation of French-

Spanish relations can be divided into three phases. During Phase I (1977-1981), each country determined its policy toward the other; Phase II (1982-1984) yielded solutions to common problems; and in Phase III (1985-1987), Paris and Madrid institutionalized their new relationship.

Phase I (1977-1981)

The starting point in the evolution of cooperation between the French and Spanish governments was the formal request made by Spain in July 1977 to join the European Community.[1] While mindful of other issues of mutual concern, especially ETA (Euskadi Ta Askatasuna) terrorism, Paris and Madrid were preoccupied first and foremost by the EC enlargement process during the first phase of their rapprochement. In fact, the question of Spanish membership in the Community would dominate bilateral affairs until January 1, 1986 when Spain joined the EC. The first step toward improved relations, however, was to grasp and diagnose the degree to which French and Spanish interests conflicted or coincided as Spain joined the ranks of Western democracies. The perceptions in Paris and Madrid of the respective sets of interests at stake were influenced by domestic political considerations within each country, bilateral diplomacy, and the impact of events.

The Domestic Debates

Two days after becoming the new Spanish head of state in late November 1975, King Juan Carlos delivered his first public address in which he made the following statement:

> The idea of Europe would be incomplete without a reference to the presence of the Spaniard and without a consideration of the activity of many of my predecessors. Europe should reckon with Spain, and we Spaniards are Europeans.[2]

The King's message was that Spain had an unequivocal historical interest in resuming its traditional role in European affairs. This was certainly one of the key factors behind the government's decision in 1977 to seek admission to the EC.

But the Spanish government was also motivated by domestic political and economic considerations. The two principal domestic priorities of successive governments during the 1977-1982 period was the consolidation of Spain's nascent democratic institutions and the modernization of the economy. Membership in the European Community, it was argued, would contribute to the achievement of both objectives: the new regime would be anchored in the club of Western democracies, and economic modernization would follow from participation in the Common Market and the Community's regional development programs. Public opinion polls in the 1979s revealed that Spaniards across the political spectrum favored accession to the EC and perceived that membership would benefit their economy.[3] The debate among Spaniards, therefore, focused not on whether to join the Community but on the conditions under which would Spain become a member. On this question, the Confederación Española de Organizaciones Empresariales (CEOE), Spain's largest and most powerful interest group for industry, was a vocal watchdog over the government throughout the entire period of negotiations between Spain and the EC.

Although the CEOE did not oppose Spanish membership in the Community, at times it adopted a somewhat hostile attitude toward the government's negotiating position. The CEOE slogan on the membership issue was "Sí a la adhesión pero no a cualquier precio."[4] CEOE leaders sought to ensure that the interests of Spanish industrial sectors were given full consideration by government officials who were viewed as all too eager to negotiate admission to the EC for political reasons. In general terms, Spain's wheat, dairy, meat, and modern industrial sectors were concerned about the potential competition from France and other Community members once trade barriers were removed. On the other hand, Spanish wine, olive oil, and fruit and vegetable producers stood to gain from the opening of the Community's vast market. This, of course, was what the French feared most.

In 1981, the CEOE issued a White Book entitled "La Empresa Española ante la Adhesión al Mercado Común." This publication presented a series of recommendations demanding that the Spanish government (1) seek an immediate or accelerated dismantling of Community barriers to Spanish imports; (2) support industry efforts to improve its competitiveness; (3) eliminate bureaucratic obstacles to Spanish exports; (4) encourage foreign investment in the country; (5) promote Spanish investment abroad; and (6) reduce government intervention in currency exchange markets.[5] The primary objective of the CEOE was to ensure that the transition periods toward Spain's full participation in the EC be parallel and of equal duration for industrial and agricultural sectors. Given the content of the CEOE's demands as well as the publicity they received, it is not surprising, as one foreign ministry official has noted, that the most difficult aspect of the accession process was the Hispano-Spanish negotiations.[6]

The debate within France was no less acrimonious. While the center-right Union pour la Démocratie Francaise (UDF), and Socialist Parties favored the Community's enlargement, the Gaullist party, Rassemblement pour la République (RPR), expressed serious reservations about its consequences; and the Communist party voiced outright opposition to the idea. During a parliamentary session at the National Assembly in December 1978, representatives of the country's four political parties debated the enlargement issue.[7] Despite assurances of the minister of agriculture, Jean François-Poncet (UDF), that there was a "general consensus, with the exception of the Communist speakers, on the principle of enlargement,"[8] the political cleavages on this issue were fully exposed. François-Poncet himself evoked the consequences of enlargement on the Community's external relations, particularly with the Maghreb and suggested that a study of the problem be undertaken as a precondition to enlargement. Socialist party leader, Francois Mitterrand, expressed his support for the enlargement based on France's obligations in accordance to the Treaty of Rome:

> Why three more countries [Spain, Portugal and Greece]? First because they requested it. The only precondition has now been met: the return to democracy . . . the enlargement . . . would yield a new equilibrium in the interest of France.[9]

Nonetheless, the Socialist leader also stated that France should impose certain preconditions to enlargement not the least of which was the organization of the markets for Mediterranean agricultural products. Mitterrand's public position on the enlargement question was especially significant given his eventual impact on the negotiations between Spain and the EC.

The Communists warned that an enlarged Community would cause serious difficulties for France's wine and fruit and vegetable sectors; destroy her steel, textile, shipbuilding and fishing industries; and aggravate the unemployment situation in the EC. The RPR spokesman, Michel Debré, was perhaps more subtle in his spoken words, but his message was every bit as clear: France should above all protect and promote her national interests. He then reminded the assembly of the potential consequences of the Community's enlargement on the nation's diplomatic, military, and commercial alignments.[10] Debré's discourse echoed a vociferous pronouncement made a week earlier by RPR leader Jacques Chirac. In what became known as "L'appel du Chochin," Chirac vigorously attacked the government's entire European policy and voiced his opposition to the enlargement process. In this infamous appeal, he made the following remarks:

> The admission of Spain and Portugal to the Community raises, for our agricultural interests as well as for the functioning of our common institutions, very serious difficulties that must be resolved in advance, to avoid aggravating an already very unsatisfactory situation. . . . That is why we say NO. No to the policy of supranationalism . . . no to the international effacement of France.[11]

The economic dimension of Chirac's theme was articulated with equal vigor by the Fédération Nationale des Syndicats d'Exploitants Agricoles (FNSEA), the most powerful agricultural lobby in France. The FNSEA argued that enlargement would add to the Community's surplus of wine, olive oil, and fruits and vegetables, thereby complicating any efforts to reform its Common Agricultural Policy (CAP).[12] More importantly, French farmers, especially those from the southwest region of the country, felt threatened by the potential of Spanish wine and fruit and vegetable producers to capture shares of their traditional and, in some cases, shrinking markets within the Community.[13] This was certainly the case for winegrowers in Languedoc and Rousillon who produce primarily inexpensive table wines. Consumption of this category of wine began to decline in France during the 1970s.[14] Furthermore, Spain could easily increase its production of similarly cheap wines given the amount of Spanish land planted with vines (1.7 million hectares).[15]

Finally, French farmers and political leaders alike were preoccupied with the difficulty the Community would encounter in absorbing citrus fruits from both Spain and Maghreb.[16] Motivated by political and strategic considerations, the EC had granted the Maghreb and Middle Eastern countries special access to its markets for their primary agricultural exports. France and other member-states of the Community were concerned that enlargement "would endanger these carefully cultivated associations."[17]

Bilateral Diplomacy

The coronation of King Juan Carlos on November 27, 1975 provided the first occasion in the post-Franco era for France and Spain to begin the process of normalizing their relations. It was an opportunity that French president Valéry Giscard d'Estaing did not miss. While in Madrid, Giscard held a personal meeting with the king and delivered a formal declaration in which he spoke of Spain's historical links to Europe. He also expressed hope that Spain would eventually join in the construction of a European political union. While he was well received in Spain, Giscard's overtures to the king and the tone of his remarks were criticized in his own country in view of the nondemocratic nature of the Spanish regime.[18] Nonetheless, there was optimism on both sides of the Pyrenees about the chances for improved relations between the two countries. There was even greater expectations of a warming trend in the relationship once democracy was formally established in Spain in December 1978 following the approval by referendum of the new Spanish constitution.

But things would prove to be messier in the actual bargaining between Paris and Madrid. This became evident during a brief visit to Paris by Spanish Prime Minister Adolfo Suárez in September 1977. Although the focus of the meetings Suárez held with President Giscard d'Estaing and Prime Minister Raymond Barre was Spain's candidacy to the EC, the Spanish prime minister also raised the delicate issue of Basque terrorism.[19] On this question the Spanish government was seeking (1) a change in French policy that permitted Basque militants to obtain asylum in France by claiming the status of political refugee; and (2) the extradition to Spain of suspected Basque terrorists held by French authorities. For several reasons, the French government was reluctant to alter its position on the Basque/political asylum issue. First, Spain had a strong authoritarian legacy and had not yet completed its transition to democracy. To many Frenchmen it would have been inconsistent with democratic principles to assist Spain to round up Basques whose activities were directed toward liberation from a nondemocratic regime. However, France could no longer credibly employ this argument after the 1978 referendum returning democracy to Spain. A second concern in France was that yielding to Spanish demands would jeopardize its proudly held status as a "land of political asylum." Thirdly, political leaders were disinclined to bend on this question because they feared that such a move would result in a negative reaction from the Basques in national elections.

The Suárez trip to Paris set the agenda and tone for subsequent meetings between leaders of the two countries. During an official visit to Madrid in June 1978, Giscard promised Spanish officials that he would actively support Spain's accession to the EC. In particular, he promised a study of the difficulties the enlargement would create for both France and Spain and suggested bilateral meetings to explore solutions to common problems. In addition, Giscard and Suárez tacitly agreed to cooperate on the Basque issue.[20] Although the summit was a success, hopes of better relations were soon dashed by heated domestic debates in both countries, especially in France, on Spain's candidacy to the Community. Moreover, Spain soon became discouraged by the lack of French action against ETA terrorism. Spain's foreign minister, Marcelino Oreja, began to demand more from France than empty words.[21] In January 1979, Oreja met with Francois-Poncet, by then minister of foreign affairs, and presented him with a list of 127 ETA terrorists who, according to the Spanish government, profited from asylum in France to launch terrorist operations across the border into Spain. He also asked the French government to cease granting political asylum to suspected Basque militants. France responded with its first concession to Spain on this issue by announcing that it would no longer permit the legal admission of political refugees from Spain.[22]

The next bilateral tête-à-tête came in November 1979 when Suárez, accompanied by five of his key ministers, made an official visit to Paris. The items on the agenda remained the same. Spanish officials pressured the French government to act on its promises and sought to obtain the extradition of certain ETA terrorists. On the enlargement question, Suárez and his ministers reminded Paris of the importance of creating around Spain an international context that would discourage attempts by the extreme Right to undermine Spanish democracy. French and Spanish officials also discussed the idea of sector-by-sector transition periods for Spain's entry into the European Community.[23] Though cordial in tone, the results of this meeting were notably inconsequential.

The Impact of Events

In the first three years of the 1980s, domestic political considerations and a series of events halted what little progress had been made in improving French-Spanish relations. Although the negotiations between Spain and the EC opened officially in February 1979, the Community was more preoccupied by wrangling among member-states over internal matters. In France, political forces were gearing up for the 1980/81 presidential campaign. Meanwhile, the political climate in Spain was deteriorating rapidly as the Suárez administration began to buckle under the realities of democratic governance.

These three seemingly isolated situations were inextricably linked. In a speech delivered on June 5, 1980 before the assembly of agricultural chambers, Giscard d'Estaing halted the negotiations between the EC and Spain and Portugal by imposing certain preconditions to the Community's enlargement.[24] In particular, Giscard demanded a resolution of the Community's budgetary difficulties and a reform of the Common Agricultural Policy. The French president was responding in part to the decision of the Council of Ministers one week earlier requesting the EC Commission to draw up proposed solutions to these problems. In some respects, Giscard was implying that British intransigence on the EC budget question led him to veto the enlargement process.[25] But his primary motivations were political. The forum he selected to announce his new position was evidence enough that Giscard was courting the farm vote for the elections in May 1981. As Francois Mitterrand remarked, Giscard had "his eyes fixed on the ballot boxes."[26] Needless to say, Giscard's pronouncement aroused a wave of anti-French sentiment throughout Spain. Prime Minister Barre attempted to mend fences with Spanish officials during a trip to Madrid one month later but was largely unsuccessful.[27]

The events in Spain were even more dramatic.[28] Prime Minister Suárez's popularity started to wane as ETA terrorism began to escalate and the economy showed little signs of improvement. By 1980, the euphoria toward democracy was replaced by a certain disenchantment among Spaniards with the transformation. Ironically, the man who had played the key role in the transition to democracy seemed paralyzed by the challenges of democratic leadership. In May 1980 the government narrowly defeated a parliamentary vote of no-confidence tabled by the Socialist opposition. More importantly, support within his own party, the Unión del Centro Democrático (UCD), began to crumble and an August 1980 poll showed an approval rating for Suárez of only 24 percent.[29] On January 29, 1981, Suárez resigned.

Within a month, the military attempted to take full advantage of what appeared to be an opportune moment to "restore order" in Spain. On February 23, 1981, Colonel Antonio Tejero and General Jaime Milans del Bosch staged a military coup to take over the country. Fortunately, the coup failed, thanks to the skillful intervention of King Juan Carlos who had the support of several military officers.

The events of F-23 are by now well known. It is important, however, to underscore the impact of this crisis on Spain's relations with France and other member-states of the Community. By revealing the fragility of Spanish democracy, F-23 altered the perception of the interests at stake in the Community's enlargement. It gave real meaning to the Spanish thesis that its new democracy required a more propitious international environment in which to be nurtured. The implications of this message for France were now readily apparent. First, the French government would have to support Spanish efforts to stem the activity of Basque terrorists. Evidence suggests that the rise in ETA terrorism was a main factor leading to the events of February 23.[30] Second, France would be pressed to override its own veto on the enlargement process. The alternative for Paris was to leave itself open to accusations that it was only concerned with protecting narrowly defined interests on matters of less significance than the viability of democracy in neighboring Spain. Francois Mitterrand, victorious in the French presidential elections of May 1981, would be faced with the challenge of reconciling French national interests with the normalization of French-Spanish relations.

Phase II (1982-1984)

In May 1982 Spain formally became a member of NATO. The government of Leopoldo Calvo Sotelo hoped that joining the alliance would improve the prospects for Spain's integration into the EC. Madrid's objective was to pressure France, both directly as well as through other member-states of the Community (especially West Germany) to remove the obstacles in the enlargement path. While motivated by national security interests and the domestic political situation, Calvo Sotelo also wanted to send a signal to Community members of Spain's desire to join the club of Western democracies.[31]

It is difficult to determine the extent to which the decision to join NATO came to influence the policy of Francois Mitterrand toward Spain. Yet the links between the stability of Spanish democracy, the enlargement of the Community, and Spain's status in NATO were now obvious to the French government. Nevertheless, the Mitterrand government was in no hurry to change its policy on the Basque issue. Despite a request from Calvo Sotelo during a visit to Paris in July 1981, France still refused to extradite Basque militants to Spain.[32] During a visit to Madrid one year later in June 1982, Mitterrand did show signs of yielding to Spanish demands concerning Basque terrorism. Though he received a cool reception in Spain, Mitterrand concluded his meetings with Calvo Sotelo and other Spanish officials on a positive note. He expressed an understanding of Spain's difficult struggle against terrorism and a desire to improve bilateral relations by promising more regular meetings between French and Spanish ministers.[33] However, cooperation between Paris and Madrid would have to await the electoral victory of the Partido Socialista Obrero Español (PSOE) in October 1982. When Felipe González became prime minister of Spain on December 3, 1982, Mitterrand had additional incentive to improve relations with Spain. A committed Socialist, Mitterrand could support Spanish democracy and, at the same time, advance socialist causes within Spain: What better moment to have Spain enjoy the fruits of European cooperation? Furthermore, despite France's independent status in NATO,[34] Mitterrand's policies were decidedly Atlanticist and the French had no interest in creating tensions with its allies over Spain's status in the alliance. Since González had promised a referendum on Spain's membership in NATO, the effect of the stalemate in the enlargement negotiations on Spanish public opinion toward the West was now a crucial matter. Besides, Mitterrand, a staunch advocate of European unification, was well aware that appearing to refuse democratic Iberia admission to the EC was politically unacceptable for any member-state. The EC, in fact, could profit from enlargement to gain some momentum lost in the integration process. Finally, Mitterrand was interested in the opportunity Spain could provide France and the Community to establish closer ties with Latin America. In this regard, Mitterrand has been as Gaullist as his predecessors: viewing his country as one with a special history and global interests, Mitterrand's foreign policy has sought to enhance the role of France in international affairs.[35]

The foreign policy objectives of the new Socialist government in Madrid were (1) to integrate Spain into the European Community, (2) strengthen ties with Latin America, and (3) promote a neutralist position in security affairs.[36] González understood that, to achieve the first objective, Spain would have to resolve its differences with France. And the prospects for achieving the second goal would improve once Spain succeeded in joining the EC. Community membership would enhance its international status, thereby stimulating greater interest among Latin American governments in establishing closer ties with Madrid. Thus, on this point, French and Spanish interests were harmonious: both Paris and Madrid viewed the Community's enlargement as the main avenue toward better relations between Western Europe and Latin America. Regarding security affairs, González and the PSOE favored a referendum on the NATO question in which they intended to encourage Spaniards to vote against membership in the alliance. France, however, had little interest in a neutralist and pacifist Mediterranean neighbor but rather in one willing to contribute to the defense of Western

Europe.[37] This was especially true under Mitterrand in view of his pro-Atlanticist position on East-West issues. Fortunately, for French-Spanish relations, González would make an 180-degree reversal on his initial position on the NATO referendum but not until he had taken full advantage of the issue to advance Spain's integration into the EC.

The change in the Socialist government's defense and security policy has received sufficient attention elsewhere.[38] The purpose here is to understand its impact on French-Spanish relations; in this regard, several events in the spring of 1983 were of particular importance. In May 1983, González made an official visit to Bonn to meet with West German Chancellor Helmut Kohl. Following the summit, González expressed his "understanding and solidarity" with NATO on its decision to deploy Pershing and cruise missiles in Europe.[39] This announcement was well received in Paris since the French government was Western Europe's strongest advocate of Euromissile deployment. More important, however, was the effect that the Bonn summit and the declaration by González would have on France's posture toward the Community's enlargement. The Federal Republic of Germany strongly favored the enlargement for political, economic, and strategic reasons. On the latter point, West Germany had every interest in Spain's remaining a member of NATO but knew that there would be no chance of a favorable vote in the promised Spanish referendum on NATO as long as Spain was not admitted to the Community.

In the spring of 1983, West Germany was in an advantageous position to advance the enlargement negotiations. She held the presidency of the EC's Council of Ministers and would soon host an important meeting of the European Council—the heads of state or governments of EC member-states. This meeting took place June 17-19 in Stuttgart. In what is referred to as the "Stuttgart Formula," the Council forged a package deal on French demands for the reform of the CAP and an increase in financial resources, British insistence on budgetary discipline, and German calls for an enlarged Community.[40] In a nutshell, Germany agreed to pay the cost of enlargement in exchange for a commitment from France to lift its veto on Spain's candidacy for EC membership. Although it is difficult to determine the effect of this German-sponsored solution on the defense policy of the Spanish government, González did eventually postpone the referendum on NATO until March 1986, two months after Spain became a member of the EC.

Although a warming trend in French-Spanish relations was already in progress, the "Stuttgart Formula" would pave the way for greater bilateral movement on the enlargement issue. The first step in the process came in January 1983 when French and Spanish ministers held two days of "seminars" (*à huis clos*) at La Celle-Saint-Cloud near Paris. This meeting signified a turning point in the relationship between Paris and Madrid. At its conclusion, Foreign Ministers Claude Cheysson and Fernando Morán held a joint press conference—an unprecedented event in French-Spanish relations— in which they stated that differences over concrete problems would be resolved because of overriding common interests on a broad range of issues. As *Le Monde* reported, "the two ministers enumerated with pleasure all that, from Latin America to the Middle East, from the Atlantic Alliance to North-South relations, converges to place Paris and Madrid on the same wavelength."[41] Finally, both ministers called on the Community to remove the obstacles to enlargement by resolving its internal squabbles.

In July 1983, French and Spanish ministers held another informal working seminar at the La Granja Palace near Segovia. The Community's enlargement dominated the meetings, attended by twelve ministers, six from each government. While the Spanish ministers criticized France for refusing to set a date for Spain's admission to the EC, the meeting concentrated more on the exchange of information for the purpose of analyzing the consequences of enlargement on bilateral economic relations. As in their first encounter, the ministers discussed at length international issues including security affairs and North-South relations. On the latter question, French Foreign Minister Cheysson stated: "We have underlined the necessity of maintaining positive relations with the South . . . which separates us from certain of our allies like the United States."[42] This was obvious reference to French and Spanish discontent not only with Washington's general policy toward the Third World but also its approach to the conflict in Central America. Although differences on the enlargement and Basque issues remained, the La Granja seminar confirmed an unequivocal "psychological thaw" in bilateral relations.[43]

The first two bilateral seminars laid the groundwork for the hard bargaining to come between Paris and Madrid. While pleased with the goodwill on the part of French officials, Spain was becoming impatient with the lack of concrete results on both the Community's enlargement and the Basque issue. Even King Juan Carlos would press Mitterrand on these issues in November 1983 during a dinner between the two heads of state at the Elysée Palace.[44] Prime Minister González raised these matters once again on December 20, 1983 during a brief visit to Paris. His rendezvous with Mitterrand came on the heels of the failure of the Athens reunion of the European Council to act upon the decision made in Stuttgart six months earlier. This was, of course, a serious setback to the enlargement process. The meeting also took place, coincidentally, during a moment of heightened violence and tensions along the French-Spanish border in the Basque region.[45] Although the details of their discussions remain sketchy, by all accounts, González persuaded Mitterrand of the potential cost to Spanish democracy of further delays in finding solutions to both the enlargement and Basque problems.[46]

Following this meeting, the tone and content of statements by French officials on Spain's candidacy to the EC were undeniably favorable. A key pronouncement was made by Mitterrand himself in a speech delivered at The Hague in early February 1984: "I wish that Europe welcomes Spain and Portugal and that she tells them so without delay."[47] The timing of this change in the French attitude toward enlargement was particularly significant since France held the presidency of the EC Council of Ministers during the first semester of 1984.

The optimism on both sides of the Pyrenees was not unfounded. At the third French-Spanish seminar held at Rambouillet in mid-February, French officials presented a detailed calendar for the enlargement negotiations. Specifically, France communicated its intention to conclude the negotiations by September 30, and proposed January 1, 1986 as the effective date for Spain's accession to the Community.[48] In June 1984 there were three key agreements on issues of bilateral concern. The first of these was a French-Spanish accord to cooperate in the struggle against Basque terrorism. The agreement, signed in Madrid by the French and Spanish interior ministers, followed the expulsion by France of seventeen Basque militants to Latin America during the previous six months. According to the agreement, France recognized that a terrorist is not a political refugee, while Spain guaranteed fair treatment to any Basques returning to the country.[49] The second agreement came a few days later when on June 19, Spain accepted the Community's proposed two-staged system (based on French demands) for the integration of its fruit and vegetable sectors into the EC.[50] French officials viewed this convergence of positions as a turning point in the enlargement process.[51] Finally, at the Fontainebleau summit in late June, the European Council succeeded in working out a compromise solution on the Community's internal reforms, thereby removing a major obstacle to the enlargement process.[52] The fact that this EC accord was consummated at a summit hosted by

Mitterrand, with France at the presidency of the Council of Ministers, was particularly pleasing to the Spanish government. Overall, this succession of accords signaled an irreversible shift toward cordiality and cooperation in French-Spanish relations.

In sum, then, during this period of the transformation of bilateral relations, France and Spain clarified the values at stake in their rapprochement and worked out solutions to common problems. Whereas the emphasis during Phase I was on narrow economic interests and electoral politics, the focus of Phase II shifted somewhat to political and strategic matters of far-reaching importance. The Spanish government took full advantage of domestic events and the security context to alter French and EC perceptions of the costs and benefits of supporting Spain's democracy.

Phase III (1985–1987)

During the final phase in the process of improving bilateral relations, France and Spain succeeded in implementing prior agreements and in establishing institutionalized cooperative arrangements. The task of implementing their agreement to conclude the enlargement negotiations was difficult, to say the least. In fact, the bargaining dragged well beyond the deadline of September 30, 1984 proposed by France. Moreover, the negotiations were at times stalled by differences between France and Spain, particularly over the issues of wine and fisheries. Despite the persistence of such difficulties, French and Spanish officials approached them as common problems to be solved by partners rather than as conflicts to be fought out by adversaries. This was clearly the case at the fourth interministerial seminar in Barcelona, in late October 1984, when French and Spanish succeeded in narrowing their differences on enlargement questions, including fisheries.[53]

Nonetheless, the resolution of outstanding issues in the enlargement would require several intense bargaining sessions, including, most importantly, an intra-EC session in December 1984 and two marathon sessions in the latter part of March 1985.[54] The first of these took place in Dublin where the European Council reached an agreement on the organization of the Community's wine market, enabling the Community to present its position to the Spanish government. At the marathon sessions in Brussels, Spanish and Community negotiators worked out the seemingly intractable details on the wine and fisheries chapters, both of which necessitated unpublicized bilateral parleys between France and Spain.[55] On March

30, 1985, the Spanish government and the European Community concluded an agreement according to which Spain would become a member of the EC on January 1, 1986.

Progress on the other areas of bilateral interest was more easily obtained. In September 1984, France agreed to the extradition of four ETA members claimed by judicial authorities in Spain. This historic step would be followed by a series of expulsions during the next three years. Cooperation between Paris and Madrid was even extended to the defense areas. Following the Barcelona seminar, Spain announced the purchase of 414 Roland missiles manufactured jointly by France and West Germany.[56] Finally, French and Spanish officials continued to express their intentions to coordinate their foreign policies, especially toward North Africa and Latin America.[57]

France and Spain began the process of formalizing their new relationship during an official visit of King Juan Carlos to Paris in July 1985. On this occasion, Foreign Ministers Roland Dumas and Francisco Fernández Ordóñez signed a common declaration establishing institutionalized means for bilateral cooperation on a broad range of issues. The declaration provided for annual summits between French and Spanish presidents, thereby placing Spain on an equal footing with Great Britian and Italy in France's external relations. The two countries also agreed to continue holding interministerial seminars on an annual basis. On the enlargement question, the two governments promised to undertake initiatives at the local and regional levels to facilitate Spain's integration into the EC. In the area of defense and security, Paris and Madrid agreed to measures with potentially far-reaching significance. Specifically, the declaration provided for (1) the formation of a strategic study group consisting of high-ranking officials from their respective defense and foreign policy establishments, and (2) the development of a joint effort in the production of military arms.[58]

Spanish officials were concerned that these new ties between Paris and Madrid would be jeopardized once RPR leader Jacques Chirac became prime minister of France. Chirac and his minister of agriculture, Francois Guillaume, had often expressed their opposition to the terms of the accession treaty between the EC and Spain and demanded its renegotiation during the campaign that preceded the RPR victory in the legislative elections of March 1986. But once in office, Chirac quietly shifted his overall position on the European Community as well as his policies toward Spain and its membership in the EC. There have been no calls for a renegotiation of the enlargement treaty. Instead, the Chirac government has continued on the course established by his Socialist predecessors. This continuity is more a function of a fundamental change in Chirac's attitude toward France's role in Europe[59] than of the cohabitation arrangement according to which Chirac shares foreign policy decisionmaking with Socialist president Mitterrand.

During the interministerial seminar in Zaragoza in October 1986, French and Spanish officials demonstrated that the trend toward cordial relations would transcend any ideological gap that may exist between them. The seminar yielded an agreement ending a contentious dispute between the two countries over fishing rights in the Bay of Biscay. The two governments also agreed to seek a solution to their differences concerning the Community's Mediterranean policies. On this issue, France favored an extension of the Community's preferential treatment of certain agricultural products imported from countries on the Mediterranean's southern littoral. Spain opposed the idea because Morocco, Tunisia, and Israel compete with Spain in the Community's citrus fruits and olive oil markets.[60] Nevertheless, Madrid agreed to withdraw its opposition to renewal following Chirac's visit to Madrid on November 6, 1986.[61]

The French government also continued to cooperate with Spanish authorities in the struggle against Basque terrorism, viewed increasingly as linked to the overall problem of international terrorism. Just four months after taking office, the Chirac government arrested a suspected member of the military organization of ETA who was living in France and placed him under custody of the Spanish police.[62] Seven more Basques were handed over to Spanish authorities in early November while Chirac and his foreign minister were on their way to meet with González and other Spanish officials in Madrid. At this meeting, the two heads of government opposed the British request for Community sanctions against Syria following revelations of Syrian involvement in several terrorist incidents in Western Europe. They agreed that such measures would risk aggravating Euro-Arab relations. Chirac and González also discussed the possibility for Spanish industry to participate in the *Ariane* and *Hermes* space projects and the newly established CGE-ITT alliance in telecommunications.[63]

In March 1987, France and Spain held their first institutional summit as provided for in the agreement of July 1985. The summit took place in Madrid and was attended by both Mitterrand and Chirac who were joined by seven French ministers. Their meetings with González and Spanish ministers focused on international rather than bilateral issues and demonstrated a clear convergence in French and Spanish views in the area of foreign policy and defense. Regarding the Soviet proposal to dismantle short-range nuclear missiles in Europe, France and Spain supported arms negotiations but agreed that any U.S.-Soviet deal on disarmament should maintain the balance of forces in Europe. Of particular significance, France communicated its support for Spanish membership in the recently revived West European Union (WEU). French and Spanish officials also called for an international conference on the conflicts in the Near and Middle East and discussed possibilities for cooperation among Mediterranean countries. Finally, Paris and Madrid expressed support for the creation of a single market among EC member-states by 1992 while Spain emphasized the importance of correcting regional disparities within the Community.[64]

In general terms, the past two French-Spanish summits have marked the beginning of a new era in relations between Paris and Madrid. There was no trace at either summit of the traditional suspicions and misunderstanding that had characterized the relationship for so many decades. Instead, the two countries have succeeded in establishing an institutionalized framework for future cooperation on a broad range of issues.

Conclusion

During the past decade, France and Spain have overcome what were primarily domestic obstacles to bilateral cooperation. The Spanish people removed the principal impediment to better relations by transforming the country's authoritarian regime into a viable democracy. The French government, for its part, realized that the fruits of closer ties with Spain outweighed the cost of any dissatisfaction among certain farm sectors and political factions who stood to lose from French-Spanish cooperation on Basque terrorism and the Community's enlargement. In the process of resolving their differences on these questions, France and Spain have laid the groundwork for further cooperation on bilateral, regional, and international issues around which other interests have converged. And, as Chirac's recent overtures to Madrid demonstrate, the convergence of French and Spanish national interests is based on the similarities of their situations in the international system and not on some temporary ideological compatibility of their respective governments. In addition to the similarity of their political regimes and geographic settings, France and Spain now share common commitments to regional and international institutions. Both are partners in the European enterprise and both have accepted the responsibility of contributing to Western security.

Through their formalized entente, Paris and Madrid have recognized opportunities for cooperation in several foreign policy areas. They have expressed an interest in working together to promote West European ties with Latin America and the Arab world. The two countries are also likely to join forces within the EC, perhaps in alliance with Italy, Greece, and Portugal, in bargaining among member-states over the Community's regional development programs, Mediterranean policy, and the CAP. And given the perceived link between the rise of international terrorism and Basque militancy, the two governments will continue to coordinate efforts to stem terrorist activity in their countries. The routine expulsion of suspected Basque terrorists to Spain by French authorities during the past year is a clear indication of their accord on this issue.[65] Finally, Paris and Madrid see eye to eye on matters of defense and security. Among NATO's sixteen members, France and Spain are the only countries that do not participate in the alliance's integrated military command structure. Moreover, French support of Spain's intention to join the WEU is further evidence of a mutual desire for greater independence from the United States in security affairs.

There are, however, structural constraints that limit the degree to which France and Spain can extend their cooperation on foreign policy matters. If Paris and Madrid intend to promote closer ties with Latin America, they will have to count on more than Spain's historical and cultural ties with the Hispanic world. They will have to persuade their European partners to develop economic and commercial links with Latin America along the lines of the Community's preferential trade agreements with the African, Caribbean, and Pacific (ACP) countries.[66] But the EC is not likely to consider a proposal of this nature any time soon. In the first place, the Community is reluctant to take any action that would exacerbate its agricultural surpluses or strain its existing trade arrangements. Moreover, such action would mean adding a potentially contentious issue to the Community's crowded agenda. Finally, it would require a protracted round of bargaining among the Twelve before the EC could undertake any negotiations with Latin America governments.

The reality of international politics will also limit the practical significance of French-Spanish cooperation in security affairs. The countries of Western Europe still depend on the United States' nuclear umbrella for their security. Thus, while France and Spain support the idea of an autonomous West European defense organization, there is no realistic alternative to NATO for the foreseeable future. Not only has NATO survived almost forty years of trans-Atlantic squabbling, it also has a much better track record than purely West European defense initiatives. The WEU, for example, is just getting back on its feet after a long period of dormancy. More importantly, government leaders in Western Europe are reluctant to decouple the theater nuclear forces in their countries from the U.S. strategic arsenal. This link in the escalation ladder reassures them of the credibility of American deterrence against Soviet aggression. Hence, the WEU may develop alongside NATO but it will not replace the alliance between the United States and Western Europe.

In conclusion, while there is every reason to expect close ties between France and Spain to continue in the near future, it is unlikely that French-Spanish cooperation will have meaningful consequences outside the bilateral and regional contexts.

Notes

The author would like to thank the Ford Foundation and The Center for International Affairs, Harvard University for their generous support during the preparation of this study.

1. Commission of the European Communities, *Bulletin of the European Communities* 7/8 (Luxembourg: EC, 1972).
2. Quoted in Paul Preston and Denis Smyth, *Spain, the EEC and NATO*, The Royal Institute of International Affairs, Chatham House Papers, no. 22 (London:Routledge & Kegan Paul, 1984), p. 24.
3. See the following studies by Rafael López Pintor: *La opinión pública española: Del franquismo a la democracia* (Madrid:Centro de Investigaciones Sociales, 1982); "En torno a las conexiones entre opinión pública y decisión política: La actitud de los españoles ante la Comunidad Económica Europea," *Revista española de la opinión pública*, no. 37 (July-September, 1974).
4. "Yes to accession but not at any price." Quoted in Antonio Alonso, *España en el Mercado Común: Del acuerdo del 70 a la Comunidad de Doce* (Madrid:Espasa-Calpe, 1985), p. 144. This study provides an excellent account of the negotiations between the CEOE and the Spanish government on Spain's entry into the European Community.
5. Confederación Española de Organizaciones Empresariales, *La Empresa española ante la adhesión al Mercado Común*, vol. 1 (Madrid:Gráficas Maravillas, 1981), p. 96.
6. Interview conducted by the author with Manuel Marín González, Spanish Secretary of State for Relations with the European Communities (1982-1985), Brussels, July 1, 1986.
7. *Le Monde*, December 17-18, 1978, pp. 13-14.
8. Ibid.
9. Ibid.
10. Ibid.
11. *Le Monde*, December 8, 1978, p. 9.
12. Preston and Smyth, pp. 10-15; on the Community's surplus of wine see D. Boubals, "La situation viticole d'un Marché commun élargi à

l'Espagne, à la Grèce et au Portugal,"*Le Monde*, September 1, 1977.
13. *Le Monde*, September 12, 1978, pp. 1.
14. Fédération Nationale des Syndicats d'Exploitants Agricoles, *Information Agricole*, no. 571, September 1985.
15. Commission of the European Communities, *Problems of Enlargement: Taking Stock and Proposals*, Supplement 8/82, *Bulletin of the European Communities* (Luxembourg, 1983), p. 15.
16. Pascal Fontaine, "Une autre Italie,"*Le Monde*, September 1, 1987, p. 2.
17. Preston and Smyth, p. 12.
18. Ramón-Luis Acuña, *Como los dientes de una sierra: Francia-España de 1975 a 1985, una década* (Madrid:Plaza & Jánes, 1986).
19. *Le Monde*, September 1, 1977, p. 3.
20. Acuña, p. 77.
21. Ibid., p. 293.
22. Ibid., pp. 76-77, 293.
23. Ibid., pp. 88-90; *Le Monde*, November 27, 1979, pp. 1, 4.
24. *Le Monde*, June 7, 1980, pp. 1, 4, 5.
25. Great Britian was demanding a reduction in its net contribution to the Community's budget. On the links between this issue and the enlargement negotiations, see the editorial entitled "Une injustice," *Le Monde*, June 7, 1980, p. 1.
26. *Le Monde*, June 10, 1980, p. 7.
27. Acuña, pp. 81-82.
28. For an excellent review of these events see Juan Pablo Fusi, "Spain: The Fragile Democracy," *West European Politics* 5, no. 3 (July 1982).
29. *El País*, August 10, 1980. Cited in Fusi, p. 237.
30. Fusi, pp. 224-226.
31. Gregory F. Treverton, "Spain: Domestic Politics and Security Policy," International Institute of Strategic Studies, *Adelphi Papers*, no. 204 (1986), pp. 10, 31-32.
32. Acuña, pp. 174-178.
33. *Le Monde*, June 23, 24, and 25, 1982, various articles.
34. On this issue, see François de Rose, "The Relationship of France with NATO," AEI *Foreign Policy and Defense Review* 4, no. 1, (1982).
35. For several perspectives on Mitterrand's foreign policy see the following: A. W. DePorte, "France's New Realism," *Foreign Affairs* 63, no. 1 (Fall 1984), pp. 144-165; Stanley Hoffmann, "Gaullism by Any Other Name," *Foreign Policy*, no. 57, (Winter 1984/85), pp. 38-57; Roy C. Macridis, "French Foreign Policy: The Quest for Rank," in Roy C. Macridis, ed., *Foreign Policy in World Politics*, 6th ed. (Englewood Cliffs, NJ:Prentice-Hall, 1985).
36. Eusebio Mujal-León, "Foreign Policy of the Socialist Government," in Stanley G. Payne, ed., *The Politics of Democratic Spain* (Chicago:The Chicago Council on Foreign Relations, 1986).
37. De Rose, p. 25.
38. See Mujal-León, Preston and Smyth, and Treverton.
39. Alonso, p. 174.
40. Alonso, pp. 164-167; 173-175; *Le Monde*, June 21, 1983, pp. 1, 3.
41. *Le Monde*, January 13, 1983, p. 1.
42. *Le Monde*, July 5, 1983, p. 4.
43. *Le Monde*, July 2, 1983, p. 4.
44. Acuña, pp. 188, 190-191.
45. *Le Monde*, December 21, 1983, p. 1; December 22, 1983, p. 11.

46. *Le Monde*, December 21, 1983, p. 1; Acuña, pp. 191-192; Alonso, pp. 181-182.
47. *Le Monde*, February 9, 1984, p. 7.
48. *Le Monde*, February 14, 1984, p. 10.
49. *Le Monde*, June 16, 1984, pp. 1, 3; Acuña, p. 299.
50. Alonso, p. 188.
51. Interview conducted by the author with Jean de Glimatsy, Political Counselor, Permanent Representative of France to the European Communities (1982-1985), Paris, July 18, 1986.
52. *Le Monde*, June 26, 1984, pp. 1, 3.
53. *El País*, October 22, 1984, pp. 1, 11, 13.
54. On the final stage of the negotiations, see Enrique González Sánchez, "Las negociaciones de adhesión de España a las Comunidades Europeas desde abril de 1984 hasta su conclusión," *Revista de Instituciones Europeas* 17, no. 2 (May-August 1985); see also Alonso, pp. 192-204.
55. Interviews conducted by the author with Roland Dumas, French Minister of Foreign Affairs (1984-1986), Paris, June 5, 1986; and Fernando Morán, Spanish Minister of Foreign Relations (1982-1985), New York, March 11, 1987.
56. Acuña, p. 199.
57. See, for example, the statements of Felipe González quoted in *Le Monde*, December 18, 1984, p. 4.
58. *Le Monde*, July 10, 1985, pp. 1, 3; July 11, 1985, p. 4.
59. On the shift in Chirac's positions on these matters, see David Housego, "Chirac quietly alters political course towards EEC," *Financial Times*, March 24, 1987, p. 3; and the editorial entitled "Coopération à la hussarde," *Le Monde*, July 22, p. 1.
60. *Le Monde*, October 7, 1986.
61. *Le Monde*, November 7, 1986, p. 4.
62. *Le Monde*, July 27, 1986, pp. 1, 8.
63. *El País*, November 7, 1986, pp. 1, 12, 15, 16. *Le Monde*, November 7, 1986, pp. 1, 4 and November 8, 1986, p. 6.
64. *Le Monde*, March 11, 12, 13, and 14, 1987, various articles.
65. Agathe Logeart, "La routine des expulsions au Pays basque français," *Le Monde*, March 12, 1987, pp. 1, 12.
66. Françoise Barthélémy, "L'Europe peut-elle jouer un rôle plus constructif en Amérique Latine?," *Le Monde Diplomatique* (January 1987).

PART 3
STRATEGIC IMPLICATIONS OF SPAIN'S ENTRY INTO NATO

7

European Socialism, the Western Alliance, and Central America: Lost Latin American Illusions

Carlos Rico F.

The Central American crisis has become a particularly interesting terrain in which to analyze some of the "new realities" that characterize relations between the United States and other Western countries in the 1980s. New realities indeed: an area of the world which until quite recently had such a low place in the agenda of international politics, U.S. foreign policy, or even interamerican relations that the assistant secretary of state for Latin American affairs in the early 1970s devoted no more than 3 percent of his time to it,[1] using it then only as a case study to characterize much wider changes. That this is even possible is a result, basically, of two developments.

The first one is related precisely to the place this area held in the context of international politics for most of this century. It was an almost undisputed North American preserve, in which other Western countries (with the exception of Britain's presence in Belize) had quite limited interests. Central America was not only the subregion of Latin America where the dominant presence of the United States was originally established but also one of the first areas of the world in which Europeans accepted a leading role on the part of the emerging new world power. Thus, while the presence of European governments and nongovernmental forces was quite open in South America during the interwar decades, the same was not the case in the isthmus, where the United States was able to develop an almost unchallenged presence even during its isolationist years. After the Second World War, while Latin America as a whole saw its international alternatives dwindle, Central America was confirmed as what I have called elsewhere an area of U.S. "hyperhegemony."[2]

The contrast between that reality and the present proliferation of international actors that, one way or another, have participated in the difficult process of transition launched by the 1979 triumph of the Sandinista National Liberation Front in Nicaragua is indeed remarkable. And what makes this relevant to understanding intra-West relations, particularly in the sphere of security perceptions, is the fact that among those new actors other Western governments, both from Europe and from Latin America, have played important roles.

The second development is in turn related to the direction that such new participation has taken. Both the governments of the largest Latin American governments and several Western European public and private forces have been openly critical of the policies pursued by the Reagan administration in the area, refusing to let the U.S. leadership role be taken for granted. This has given rise to an interesting paradox: At the same time that the U.S. government publicly bases its policy prescriptions to deal with the crisis on the defense of Western interests that it says are threatened by the Soviet Union and its allies, those other governments whose interests are also supposedly being defended refuse to share that perception of threat. In fact, those other Western countries seem at times to have perceived threats to their interests that emanate not from Soviet actions but from U.S. behavior in the area.

From a Latin American perspective there are other reasons, not directly connected to the problem of security perceptions but equally compelling, to carefully examine the extent of European involvement in the Central American crisis. They are in turn related to the possibility of taking that crisis, for precisely the same reasons that I have already summarized, as an example of the more general trends towards a more polycentric international order in which new alternatives may be open for them. Since at least the end of the 1960s, most goverments of the region have attempted, with diverse results, to "break out" of the Western Hemisphere and develop new alternatives that may increase their international bargaining power.[3]

These Latin American efforts to "diversify dependency" have been widely chronicled. Two limitations of most of this literature must be noted in connection with the topic of this paper. In the first place, the emphasis has usually been put on the economic dimensions of the diversification efforts. Second, increases in contacts between the region and extrahemispheric powers are usually seen as the result of Latin American initiatives. Important aspects of the problem are thus frequently overlooked. Such is the case of the political dimensions of the diversification, not only in terms of the posibilities for restricted political alliances with governments beyond the Western Hemisphere, but also in terms of the contacts and mutual support that may be developed between different political forces of various Western countries. A second dimension not always adequately covered is related to the role that those alternative poles of relation, in this case the Europeans, may play (and have played in some instances) in the context of rapprochement efforts.

This discussion tries to look at European involvement in Latin American affairs and its implications for perceptions in the sphere of security by taking the Central American crisis as an example of the potential disagreements that may crop up among Western countries in that issue area. With this in mind I focus my attention on a set of European political actors that are, at the same time, squarely within the parameters of what we may define as "the West," and most likely to place a different emphasis in their examination of security-related questions: European social democrats. In examining them I will concentrate most of my attention on the international forum in which they participate (the Socialist International), but I will also make some references to specific actions by national parties and even by governments in those cases where socialist parties have been in power during the years of the Central American crisis.

The basic theme I will develop is centered on the expectations that the activism of some of these forces awakened both in Europe and in Latin America, in terms of its potential for creating a bridge between Latin American security perceptions and the key concerns shared in that issue area by the main participants in the Western alliance.

I take three steps in presenting my argument. The first step recapitulates the main antecedents to the European socialist's involvement in the Central American subregion and more generally in Latin American affairs. The second step summarizes the main reasons that account for the expectations that were raised as a result of that participation. The third step examines the role of European socialists in the context of the Central American crisis, focusing on their disagreements with the Reagan administration. Finally, I present a preliminary evaluation of the present state of European social democrat activities in connection with the Central American crisis and the potential for some increased participation by them in other issue areas and other parts of the region. Thus, after devoting the body of the discussion to recording the main reasons that may be given to justify the hopes raised by such increased activism in the area, I concentrate my final considerations on the subsequent dampening of those expectations.

European Socialist Parties and Latin America: From the Years of Solitude to Increased Attention in Times of Crisis

In a well-known process, which has its roots in the mid-nineteenth century and in particular in the creation of the Second International in 1889 and its later development, European political forces that posited socialism as their objective gradually became divided into two main currents. The communist movement, the first one of those currents, was increasingly perceived after the Russian Revolution of 1917 to be closely tied to what was to become the main international competitor of the United States and as such attracted a fair deal of attention of students of international relations.

The second current, social democracy, attracted less attention among international relations scholars, particularly in the United States. It was formed by those political parties and movements which, in their original thinking, argued that socialism could be achieved through the reform of capitalism, and which placed high value in the preservation and expansion of the political achievements of liberal democracy. Gradually these forces came to emphasize the reform of existing social, economic, and political structures rather than their radical transformation.

Both these movements developed international connections in other parts of the world. However, an interesting difference between them became apparent in the first decades of the twentieth century in terms of their ability to take root in the less developed areas of the planet. While communist ideology developed in parts of Asia and Latin America, social democracy remained basically a European phenomenon despite the efforts of different metropolitan socialist parties to promote the creation of like-minded political movements in the European colonies of the day.

This basic difference is particularly apparent in Latin America. According to one of the foremost historians of socialist thought, the region did not play an important role in any of the branches of the socialist movement at least until after the First World War.[4] However, by the second decade of this century several communist parties were active in the area. On the other hand, for most of this century there has been only a very small number of parties formally affiliated with those organizations in which social democrats have joined forces. The most prominent exceptions to this situation in the early decades of the century were the socialist parties of Argentina and Uruguay which, after participating in the activities of the Second International, maintained their limited connections with their European counterparts. Political forces from both Brazil and Chile sporadically participated in those international efforts.[5]

The difficult period social democracy went through from the beginning of the First World War until the mid-1940s can be seen as one of the causes of that situation. The reorganization of the international social democratic movement that culminated in 1951 with the creation of the Socialist International prepared the ground for a new period of international activity by European social democratic parties, several of which came to power in their respective countries. Such potential, however, was not fully developed until some years later.

The attempt to find a "third way" between the dominant socioeconomic systems of the postwar world and the mixture of political liberalism, social and economic reformism, and quite open anticommunism that characterized the early statements of principles of the organization had a double impact. On the one hand, they alienated a good part of socialist forces in the world, which tended to perceive social democrats as too close to U.S. positions in the cold war confrontation; on the other hand, they attracted the attention of several political forces in the underdeveloped areas of the world that were themselves trying to gain some distance from both superpowers.

The force of this attraction and the priority that social democrats gave to expanding it were limited during the 1950s and 1960s by three sets of factors: (1) the perceived alignment of European socialism behind the United States; (2) the position taken by several European socialist parties during the process of decolonization, which dominated North-South relations during that period; and (3) the fact that during those years the problems of European reconstruction were at the top of the list of priorities of most political forces in that area of the world.

Two different developments took place as those limiting circumstances changed. In the first place, once decolonization was basically completed and the cold war started to melt down, the potential appeal of the key aspects of European social democratic thinking for other regions of the world became increasingly apparent. Second, as their economic woes lessened, Europeans began to devote more attention to relations with countries of the underdeveloped world other than their own colonies. A happy coincidence of circumstances took place and the efforts formally introduced by the Socialist International to stop being only "western and white"[6] found a much better ground for expression under those conditions. In the next section I will summarize some of the more specific reasons why

European social democracy appealed to important segments of the Latin American political spectrum as a potential element in their international activities. At this point my interest is in recording the slow process of increased relations between European social democracy and Latin American political forces.

The road to increased Latin American participation in social democratic international activities was long. Not only did relatively few political forces in the region openly share the stated thinking of the movement, but during the 1950s and 1960s European social democratic parties concentrated their limited efforts on developing a "Third World constituency" in their former colonies. Such efforts, on the other hand, were to bear very limited fruits, which in turn became one of the reasons for the attention paid to Latin America in later years.

When the Socialist International was created in 1951 only two political parties of the region, again those of Argentina and Uruguay, were listed among its members.[7] Jamaican socialists joined the International in 1952, and in 1955 a Latin American secretariat of the organization was established in Montevideo,[8] in which the Chilean Popular Socialist party also participated. According to Felicity Williams, in its first six years the secretariat was "in touch" with the Socialist parties of Brazil, Ecuador, Panama, and Peru, Colombia's Popular Socialist party, Cuba's Socialist Federation and the 26th of July movement, Venezuela's Democratic Action, Costa Rica's National Liberation party, Peru's Alianza Popular Revolucionaria Americana (APRA), Bolivia's Movimiento Nationalista Revolutionario (MNR), Paraguay's Partido Revolucionario Febrerista, the Dominican Republic's United Front, in exile, and diverse European exile communities in Mexico.[9]

All this, however, did not bring noticeable changes to a situation characterized by the almost total lack of interest on the part of the European socialist parties in relation to the 1954 coup in Guatemala and the denounced U.S. participation in that event.[10] The Latin American secretariat tried to steer a middle course between military dictatorships, which in many cases were openly supported by the United States and the communist parties of the region whose militants were increasingly influenced by the example of the Cuban revolution after 1959. This was not easy in the context of the sixties, when the impact of the Cuban revolutionary process, on the one hand, and the commitment of many reformist forces to the U.S.-sponsored Alliance for Progress, on the other, left a very limited space to social democrats who would emphasize a European connection.

It is, however, in the context of the early 1960s that political parties from four Latin American countries (Costa Rica, Paraguay, Peru, and Venezuela) joined the International as observers, showing an increase in interest which led to the transformation of the Latin American secretariat into a liaison bureau in 1966. By the end of that decade Latin American parties linked to the organization constituted its second largest geographic component.

It was during the late sixties that the increased attention paid by the European social democrats to relations with the developing world picked up speed. Several factors were involved in that change. A first element was the modified tone of international politics introduced by the German Federal Republic's ostpolitik. In this sense a second element that it seems necessary to bring into the analysis is related to the resurgence of the Sozialdemokratische Partei Deutschlands (SPD) in the politics of its own country in the late sixties.

West Germany had two characteristics that helped it develop a leading role in the "Third World policies" of the Socialist International. The first one was related to the key role that German socialists had played in the movement in the years when it was still a part of the Second International. This leading role was confirmed with the influential participation that the SPD had in the process of revising social democratic ideology in the early fifties. Its Bad Godesberg program made public in 1951 was very influential in recreating the International during the same year. The second factor had to do with the lack of former colonial possessions—a characteristic the Germans shared with their Northern European counterparts—which imposed relatively fewer constraints in their behavior in relation to that of countries such as France or Great Britain.

The West Germans also gave several examples of the disagreements important components of European social democratic parties have had with different aspects of U.S. foreign policy. On the other hand, those disagreements, which were also to have an important role in the increased activism of the social democratic parties, basically expressed concerns that were relevant in other countries as well. Thus, the role that the German social democratic youth (the Jusos) played in prompting their party to a more activist role in "Third World affairs" was clearly influenced by an event that had an important impact in youth movements throughout the world: the Vietnam war.

Other factors pushed in the same direction. In the context of the international economic difficulties of the early seventies, and in particular as a result of the first energy crisis, European governments, many of which were then under the control of social democratic parties, intensified the attention they paid to "Third World matters."

There were other, more particular, reasons for the increased attention. European governments' emphasis on a kind of reformist welfare-statism seemed at that point to be domestically more viable in Latin America than in other areas of the underdeveloped world. This reflected the perception that some countries in the region were approaching the ranks of a "middle class of nations," for which economic restrictions on reformism would be less acute. Even on purely economic grounds there were reasons for Latin America to attract European attention well beyond social democratic circles. The region was seen at the same time as a vast potential market, the most industrialized region of the developing world, an area rich in mineral and energy resources, and a potential supply of relatively qualified but cheap labor.[11] And if all this was not enough, Latin America itself was committed to developing alternative poles of relations beyond the Western Hemisphere and, for reasons that I will discuss in the next section, considered the European social democrats as an attractive option.

Three other factors contribute to the picture. The more general assertion of European interests during those years vis-à-vis the United States also contributed to the increase in reciprocal interest. The flexibility with which the International began to approach such thorny issues as the notion of political democracy that members had to abide by certainly eased matters even more; this was particularly so in relation to political parties that had their roots in populist movements that some European socialists saw as related to their own experiences with fascism. Finally, the important role that the socialist parties of Spain and Portugal started to play in Socialist International circles after the fall of the last remnants of European fascism added a new element to the attention that Latin America could expect to receive in those same circles.

In the early 1970s all these developments had created a set of very favorable conditions for the rapprochement between European social democracy and those forces one could associate with Latin America's "democratic Left." The 1971-1973 experience of the Popular Unity government in Chile was the final element needed to catalyze that interest. Several aspects of the Chilean experience contributed to increasing European social democratic interest in Latin America. Chile's "electoral road to socialism" had attracted the attention of socialist political forces worldwide, practically from the moment of Allende's triumph.

For the social democrats it assumed a particularly important meaning since it seemed to prove that peaceful processes of transition were possible even in less developed areas of the world. Since "la vía chilena" openly aimed at not only reforming existing structures but at "building socialism" itself, it also tended to capture the imagination of European political actors who perceived themselves as constrained by the political realities of their own countries from going "that far." The appeal of the Chilean experiment for these forces had several concrete expressions. Thus, the first time that the Bureau of the Socialist International met on Latin American soil was in February 1973 in Santiago de Chile.

The assassination of President Allende, the September 1973 coup, and the level of repression in the country in the wake of those events galvanized the attention not only of European socialists but of wider segments of European and world public opinion. The Church Commission's U.S. Senate investigation on the role of the U.S. government in the destabilization of the Chilean government, in turn, increased the gap in the security perceptions of U.S. political elites and significant parts of the European political spectrum which saw many parts of the Chilean deposed coalition as their own. The words that Américo Ghioldi, exiled member of the Argentine Socialist party, had used in his report on Latin America to the 1955 International Socialist Congress would find a more receptive audience almost twenty years later: "With pathetic blindness that great country [the United States], claiming strategic reasons, has provided arms to dictators who use them against their own peoples."[12]

In more than one sense, the Chilean fight against a military dictatorship supported by the United States took on for a new generation of European socialists the flavor of something similar to the anti-fascist struggles that those social democratic militants who were by then in charge of both the movement and their national parties had fought a quarter century before in their own countries. As other South American countries joined Chile on the road to authoritarianism, the International's scope of attention on Latin America was widened.

In the second half of the 1970s Latin America was second only to Europe itself as the area where the Socialist International had more contacts, and its importance increased in the agenda of a movement that declared itself committed to changing its well-deserved eurocentric image. The last years of the decade witnessed a series of high-level meetings between important leaders of the movement and their Latin American counterparts, as well as the extension of Latin

American participation in such political forces as Mexico's Partido Revolucionario Institucional (PRI), Brazil's Movimento Democrático Brasileiro (MDB) and El Salvador's Movimiento Nacionalista Revolucionario (MNR). The elections in the Dominican Republic at the end of the decade provided the International with a first case in which the possibility of concrete actions beyond declarations was validated.[13]

The Fourteenth Congress of the International, held in Vancouver, Canada in November 1978, represents the high-water mark of the Socialist International's Latin American involvement prior to the Central American crisis. Over twenty Latin American political parties and movements attended the congress, among them the Sandinista National Liberation Front.[14] This in a sense symbolized the role that the subregional conflict would play as a key stimulus to those tendencies towards a greater European socialist involvement in Latin American issues that I have summarized. The crisis, in fact, became the new focus of European social democratic activities in the region during the eighties. Before examining the role of European social democrats in Central America, however, I will present some of the factors that contributed, on the Latin American side, to giving those efforts a warm welcome.

Too High Hopes? Latin American Expectations and European Social Democracy

Within Latin America's efforts at diversification Western Europe has occupied a very important place—economically, particularly regarding trade, but even more so politically. This is a reflection of both the perception that Latin American political elites have of themselves and their countries as belonging to Western culture and civilization and of an extremely important reality: The terms of political debate in the region have interesting parallels with those that dominate in Europe. The reception given to European social democratic activities in the area has to be framed in this context.

Laurence Whitehead has pointed out how the differences between the U.S. government and the governments of Western Europe in terms of their "contrasting histories, their distinctive geopolitical roles, and their present differences of political structure...give rise to marked variations of conduct and motive."[15] Without trying to take the comparison too far it may be proposed that key terms of political debate are more similar between Europe and Latin America than between Latin America and the United

States. Thus, in each case there is both a tradition of more Burkean conservatism and an active presence of Marxism as an important component of the worldviews of important segments of their public debate.

As a result of these factors it frequently seems to be easier for Latin Americans to interact politically with European countries than with the United States, or even with nations such as Japan that in fact may be seen as very important poles of relations in the economic sphere. One aspect of all this is particularly relevant in connection with the attitudes of European social democrats in the Central American crisis. Even if social democratic parties have many times abandoned Marxism in their official declarations, the conceptual framework of the Marxist school of thought is not alien to the mindsets of many among their own militants. This often helps in the development of a more understanding attitude vis-à-vis movements in other countries that may use Marxist language, in particular as compared to the language American political elites usually use. European social democrats seem to be better disposed to separating rhetoric from reality in those cases, especially if their own former colonies are not involved.

There are other reasons for the optimism with which European actions were received in "democratic Left" circles in Latin America. The link between the lessening of East-West tensions in the early 1970s and the increasing appeal of social democracy as an international movement is particularly important to note in the context of this discussion. It is, in fact, interesting to point out that both détente and the renewed international activism of the Socialist International in "Third World affairs" were closely tied to the same individual who played a key role in their launching, first as foreign minister and chancellor of the German Federal Republic and, after 1976, as chairman of the Socialist International: Willy Brandt.[16]

The particular situation of Latin America in relation to both European decolonization and the East-West conflict gave a clearly dominant role to developments that took place in the second of those issue areas. After all, with the exception of some Caribbean islands and parts of Latin America's Atlantic coast, which have been perceived both by international observers and by Latin Americans themselves as constituting separate realities, the problems associated with European colonization had been settled much earlier. Europeans can therefore maintain a more relaxed attitude in relation to events that take place in Latin America rather than in their own spheres of immediate influence, and the impact of this situation should not be discounted.

In my opinion, however, more weight should be assigned to the easing of East-West tensions in the late sixties and early seventies. The bipolar realities of the postwar world had had a particularly peculiar impact on Latin America, where being a part of the Western world, and also the United States' "backyard," often seemed to be two sides of the same coin. This was, of course, particularly bothersome to those political forces that were at the same time committed to reform and national self-determination and committed to essentially capitalist development programs. Finding alternatives, economic and political, *within the West* became an increasing concern for them. And once the automatic alignment of European social democracy with the United States on most international issues crucial to the region was removed in the context of détente, finding alternatives became increasingly attractive to those same forces.

In addition, European economic presence was limited[17] and in fact was seen more as an alternative to U.S. complete domination than as a threat to sovereignty or national control over economic resources. This tended to diminish the concerns that the previous history of European economic involvement in the area may have raised. As Jenny Pearce has put it: "Latin America's traditional economic and political dependence on the United States and the strong resentment this has created within the region, have encouraged many to look positively toward European involvement."[18] Thus, even if the substance of European activities in the region was no different from U.S. involvement, the evaluation that Latin American elites made of the European activities tended to emphasize their positive dimensions. But other factors were involved in this welcome.

There was a perception, for example, that the Europeans were more willing to accommodate Latin American concerns in key areas of interest to the region than the United States had proven to be. Some antecedents in this regard dated back to the early 1970s and the economic negotiations that dominated North-South relations during those years. I have already referred to the increased attention to "Third World issues" that the economic problems of the early seventies helped spark on the part of European social democrats. Looked at from the other side of the table, that participation raised some expectations. Many of those expectations were connected to the fact that some of the European governments who took a leading role in North-South negotiations, in particular the social democratic governments, adopted a conciliatory tone that clearly contrasted with the first responses of the Nixon and Ford administrations in the United States to the demands of the developing countries. That response raised Latin American expectations regarding the role that European social democrats could play in the region's efforts to attain a more balanced set of international connections.

Some of the reasons behind the difference between European social democratic attitudes and those of U.S. elites are not difficult to point out. The kind of reformist welfare-statism promoted by the social democrats made them more pliable to demands for a "new international economic order," which dominated North-South discussions in the early seventies and took the place that the struggle for decolonization had earlier held in that regard. In addition, several of the social democratic parties headed the governments of countries that had had a very limited colonial experience and carried fewer legacies from such a history. The role that the Northern European parties played in the global context of those negotiations can be related to this factor.

Latin America had played, through countries such as Brazil, Mexico, and Venezuela, an important role in reform efforts, and the attitude of compromise taken by the most important European social democratic leaders in such forums as the Brandt Commission was well received in the region.[19]

A second area in which the perceptions of European social democrats seemed to clearly differ from those of U.S. political elites was related to the question of economic, social, and political change in the area, and particularly to the sources and likely direction of such change. European social democrats tended to give more emphasis to the nationalistic aspects of those struggles than their North American counterparts. Such differences were openly aired in a letter to Willy Brandt by Swedish social democrat Olof Palme. That letter summarized the view of the "U.S. connection" in relation to the Chilean coup of the early 1970s that came to prevail in social democratic circles but clearly had wider implications:

> The United States seem unable to understand and face in a constructive fashion the process of liberation which is already underway in the Latin American subcontinent. The position taken by the Americans in relation to the struggle of the Latin American peoples for freedom is as narrowminded and myopic as the one they took in the cases of China and Vietnam with people like Mao Tse Tung and Ho Chi Minh. The United States always feel threatened when a poor people fights for its national and social liberation, but that liberation is both necessary and unavoidable.[20]

A third area of differing perceptions between the United States and European social democrats tended to bring the latter nearer the viewpoints of the Latin American "democratic left." Its subject matter was the weight and interpretation that should be given to Soviet actions with regard to Third World instability. At least in part that disagreement reflected the different international roles of the different allies. European social democrats tended to take a "regionalist" view, while the U.S. government—in a tendency that was reinforced at the beginning of the Reagan administration—favored a more "globalist" one. The basic differences between the two views have been adequately summarized by Karel E. Vosskuler:

> The regional approach accepts and values the continuing diffusion of power, appreciates the unique nature of the various regional alignments, assumes rather limited objectives behind Soviet policies in most Third World areas, relies heavily upon diplomatic and economic initiatives, favours maximum dissociation from regional conflicts and relies rather more on multilateral diplomacy, particularly within the framework of the United Nations...the globalist approach...tends to situate Third World conflict in an East-West context, assumes global aspirations on the part of the Soviet leadership, relies heavily on military force, attaches great value to formal alliances and, at the same time, shows a preference for bilateral diplomacy.[21]

A last area in which Latin American and European perceptions would come close in the context of the Central American crisis was, in turn, related to the similar roles that the largest Latin American countries and some of their European counterparts played as "medium powers" in international politics. This was particularly important in relation to the emphasis they put on the value of international law and on accepted principles of international behavior as constraining factors of superpower activity, factors that would become particularly relevant as the "low-intensity warfare" directed at the Sandinista regime heated up in the mid-eighties.

As can be seen, there were interesting antecedents to the position that European social democrats were to take in relation to the Central American crisis. The description of that position constitutes the focus of the discussion that follows.

Romancing the Revolution: European Socialism and the Central American Crisis

There are some more specific background elements to the kinds of positions taken by European social democrats in connection with the

Sandinista revolution and, more generally, the Central American crisis. The first set is related to the fact itself that Central America is an area of the world where there are practically no European vital interests at stake. The second, in turn, relates to the initial response by parties affiliated with the Socialist International to the Cuban revolution in the late 1950s. In that instance most of them reacted quite positively, even if, with the increased radicalization of the process, the initial enthusiasm tended to wane after 1961. Those social democratic forces that in Europe and elsewhere kept an open mind in relation to the Cuban revolution often based their positions on the perception that such a process of radicalization and the growing ties that the Cuban revolution established with the Soviet bloc were the result of misguided policies on the part of the U.S. government.

A final set of background elements that must be taken into account is related to the role that different Central American political actors and issues had played in the activities of the Socialist International even before the Sandinista revolution. I will call these "Central American background elements." The difficult balances that European social democracy has had to maintain in the context of the crisis were in a sense announced by the kinds of connections it developed over the years in the subregion.

I have already mentioned the fact that Costa Rica's Liberación Nacional had become an observer in the International as of 1966. The Costa Rican party had established a School of Political Education for young Latin American political leaders and union officials in 1959, which in 1968 changed its name to Centro de Estudios Democráticos de América Latina and became increasingly linked to the West German social democratic foundation, the Friedrich Ebert Stiftung. Liberación Nacional had become, even before the explosion of the Central American crisis, one of the most important Latin American associates of the International.

A second Central American background element is related to the political support that European social democrats gave to the anti-Somoza struggle in Nicaragua. During the late 1970s the Somoza dictatorship in Nicaragua, along with the military regimes of Guatemala, had become preferred targets for the social democrats, who tended to see them as the worst examples of the mistaken policies that the United States was perceived as pursuing in Latin America as a whole. The Thirteenth Congress of the International, which took place in late 1976, condemned human rights abuses in Guatemala and Nicaragua, as well as in Argentina, Bolivia, Chile, the Dominican Republic, Paraguay, and Uruguay.

Nicaragua caught an increasing share of attention as the situation of that country deteriorated at the end of the decade. Venezuela's Acción Democrática and Costa Rica's Liberación Nacional contributed to this focus on Nicaragua. During 1978 the Socialist International demanded the cessation of "all arms shipments for the Somocista forces, in particular those coming from the United States" and offered "the support of its member parties for those groups within Nicaragua which are resisting the Somoza government as well as immediate assistance to a succesor government in its task of reconstruction."[22]

A final Central American background element makes reference to the fact that important figures of the Salvadoran democratic Left, which after the disappointing performance of the first two military juntas created in that country after the October 1979 coup joined the armed insurgents, had become by the late seventies formal officials of the organization.[23] The incorporation of the MNR as an observer in the Socialist International, another point of contact between those components of the Salvadoran democratic Left that joined the armed insurrection and European social democrats, has already been mentioned.

With this series of factors as a backdrop it is not surprising that European socialists were among the first international actors to rejoice in the Sandinista triumph and to offer material and political assistance to the Sandinista government; that the murders of Guatemalan opposition leaders, such as Manuel Colom Argueta, who had developed close ties to various European social democratic leaders reaffirmed the latter's interest in the region; that some of them originally took a quite sympathetic view of the Salvadoran insurrection; or that, as the conflict between Costa Rica and Nicaragua became more open, those leaders had to search for ways to balance their commitments in the area.

Three different kinds of actors have played important roles in terms of European socialist presence in the Central American crisis: governments that at different points have been under the control of socialist political forces, political parties, and, finally, the Socialist International itself. The social democratic forces of various European countries have tended to rely on each one of these channels to different degrees. Recounting all the instances of their activity in the isthmus would be not only too lengthy but also unnecessary for the purposes of this discussion. I will recall only some of the most important instances in order to illuminate the different security perceptions that these actors brought to bear in the context of the crisis.

How far we are from the indifference of 1954 becomes quite

clear when we focus on the actions of European governments in the context of the present Central American conflict, in particular those governments under the control of social democratic parties. Two types of activity deserve special attention. The first one is related to the different programs of assistance aimed at keeping open the options of the Sandinista revolution and the Salvadoran insurgents. European socialist governments participated in the initial efforts to finance the reconstruction of the Nicaraguan economy after the revolution. The Socialist government of France went so far as to provide the Sandinista regime with U.S.$15 million in arms.[24]

Social democrats were also among the primary moving forces in the launching of the dialogue, started in San José, Costa Rica in September 1984, that led to a new program of economic assistance to Central America on the part of the European Community. The levels of aid involved in that program are quite limited, and the economic relations that Central America maintains with the Europeans are not too different from those it has with the United States in qualitative terms, [25] but their political significance cannot be overlooked. The program, for example, formally included Nicaragua, in open disagreement with U.S. preferences which at that point were clearly directed at isolating the Sandinista regime.

The second area of governmental activity refers to more political kinds of support. The French Socialist government was, again, particularly active in this respect in the early stages of the crisis. In this case, an important example, not only for its own significance but also for the fact that it constitutes one of the most controversial instances of European-Latin American collaboration in the context of the crisis, is the joint communiqué that the French government issued with its Mexican counterpart in August 1981 regarding the civil war in El Salvador. In that communiqué both governments gave the Salvadoran FDR-FMLN the status of "representative political forces" and asked that the Frentes be a party to any attempt to solve the civil war in that country. This represented the high point in the participation of both the Mexican and the French governments in the Salvadoran conflict. It was criticized by several Latin American countries as intervention in the domestic affairs of that Central American country. But it also served as the starting point for a series of resolutions passed by the United Nations in the following years that called on the Salvadoran government to negotiate with the Frentes. In 1982, for example, the governments of France, Denmark, Greece and the Netherlands sponsored one such resolution that called for talks before the elections scheduled for that same year.[26]

Other examples of French actions that represented significant departures from previous European attitudes in Central America can be cited. Significant for Latin America, since it involved a reaction to U.S. activities in the area, was the offer made by President Mitterrand to help the Nicaraguan government remove the mines that had been laid in the Gulf of Fonseca by the *contras* with the support of U.S. intelligence services.

A final expression of disagreement between the European socialist governments and the U.S. government was related to the degree of support that the former gave to the process of Contadora, initiated in early 1983 by Colombia, Mexico, Panama, and Venezuela as an alternative to Reagan administration policies in Central America.[27] For example, the European governments have invited the Contadora governments to their meetings with the Central Americans aimed at establishing the program for economic cooperation referred to earlier in this discussion.

Not only the governments but also the parties and the International itself have expressed their support for the Contadora process and provided, for example through the activities of the Ebert Foundation, Western options for the Central American revolutionaries. But perhaps an even more interesting aspect of the activities of these other nongovernmental actors is related to the role they have played in generating, and making public, alternative diagnoses and policy prescriptions to deal with the crisis. The most open differences with the U.S. interpretation of the roots and potential solutions to the Central American crisis was, in fact, presented at the level of party activity. Important political figures of European social democracy presented impassionate arguments for an alternative policy, which in some instances seemed to reflect a positive, and almost idealized, view of the revolutionary processes that were taking place in the region.

A case in point is that of Swedish foreign minister Pierre Schori's book *El desafío europeo en Centroamérica*,[28] published in Sweden in 1981 and in Costa Rica the following year. Schori presents basic themes that will dominate European social democratic visions of the crisis during its early years in some of the clearest language ever used by these political forces. A first component of the vision he presents is an awareness of the historical roots of present conflicts and of the role of nationalism and national liberation in them. "The history of the Caribbean," he states early in his book, "is the history of the fight of the empires against the peoples of the region, as well as of the internal drive of those empires to eliminate one another. But it is also the history of the struggle of the Caribbean natives to liberate themselves from their foreign masters."²⁹ This emphasis on nationalism and its impact on the Central American revolutions will repeat itself, in very different tones, in practically all important statements that European social democrats will make in relation to the crisis.³⁰ Schori, however, goes further than most of those statements by linking the historical past of the region to present problems. Thus, he finishes his first chapter with a series of statements that could have come from forces much further to the Left in the political spectrum of either Europe or Central America:

> Empire builders of the modern age seem to have inherited many of the prejudices of the first colonialists. They consider Latin Americans as unable to determine their own destiny. They firmly maintain that any effort of political and economic emancipation feeds on foreign countries and ideologies and that, as a result, it is necessary to save these nations for the "free world," even if this has to be done against their will and by the force of arms. This is, in great measure, what puts the peoples of Central America today in the eye of the storm.³¹

Throughout the book the references to the United States as the main obstacle to the self-determination of Central America and one of the main components of the present crisis are almost continuous. It is in fact difficult to choose quotes. What follows is an almost random selection:

> In those cases where the national puppets have not been able to repress popular revindications for reform the new colonial power has not vacillated in intervening directly. We saw it in Guatemala in 1954 and we are seeing it this year in El Salvador.³²

> The revolutionaries found much inspiration in the rebels of previous generations. But the main motor for their actions was, of course, the situation of their own country and not the result of opinions imported from Moscow or Havana. On the other hand, measures and decisions taken in the United States, the big neighbor of the Central Americans, have an immense role.³³

> The shark has eaten many sardines throughout the years. In the history of the U.S. Marine Corps 180 cases of intervention between 1800 and 1934 are mentioned.³⁴

> Communism is not and has never been an important force in Latin America...in practice only a reactionary policy on the part of the United States can create possibilities for communism... History

clearly shows that Latin America's struggle for liberation is not an extension of the East-West confrontation. The majority of the peoples of Central America do not know and are not likely to want any communism. They want today what they wanted seventy years ago: land and liberty.[35]

When are they going to understand that the identification with the most reactionary regimes of Latin America is counterproductive and that a sustainable anti-Soviet strategy requires an attempt to lay bridges to governments which have popular support?[36]

The tone itself of such statements is interesting. It is hard to find the same kind of language in other European social democratic statements, and it is doubtful that many among them would endorse the language used. But the open contradiction they announce with the interpretations of the sources of instability that the Reagan administration brought to bear in the conflict was widely shared in social democratic circles.[37] It is easy to see why the basic assumptions of the initial public statements of the U.S. government, which tended to put the blame for the conflict on Soviet-Cuban activities, was seen by European social democratic forces not only as unrealistic but also as self-serving. And without accepting that basic diagnosis of the roots of crisis in Central America it was very difficult for them to share the prescriptions proposed to deal with it. The emphasis on military measures was thought to be misguided since it did not address the real sources of the conflict; isolating Nicaragua was perceived as shortsighted, since that country was not seen as already a part of the Soviet camp, and therefore the best way to avoid that result was to keep its options open within the West.[38]

It must be stressed that these were points espoused not only by the left wing of the movement. They represented a much wider consensus which in fact went beyond the social democratic ranks in Europe. A final point that made them all the more relevant for the topic of this discussion was that they represented disagreements with the U.S. government over means rather than policy objectives. Wolf Grabendorff has adequately summarized the complex mix of basic agreement in terms of the aims to be pursued and disagreement on the best means to achieve them that has characterized the security perceptions of European social democrats on the one hand, and the Reagan administration on the other. According to him, there is basic agreement among most European political forces and their North American counterparts in relation to the following interests:

- to prevent the Central American countries from adhering to the socialist bloc;
- to avoid regional and internal instability due to interstate or intrastate violence;
- to guarantee economic cooperation through the support of free market economies; and
- to further economic development and social justice through bilateral and multilateral aid programs.[39]

These shared interests, however, do not change the basic reality that there are significant disagreements among these partners in the Atlantic alliance, on the diagnoses of the crisis. From the European social democratic view the crisis is best characterized as

- a North-South problem in and of the Western Hemisphere;
- a problem deeply rooted in the historical relationship of the United States with its southern neighbors;
- a test case for the United States to come to terms with the solution of its informal empire;
- a test case for the Western powers to deal with revolutionary change and self-determination in the Third World;
- a problem of how to restrain the military engagement of the Soviet Union and/or radical Third World states; and
- a problem of how to avoid a superpower confrontation in the region and the resulting spillovers.[40]

As I have emphasized earlier, those different diagnoses in turn lead to different emphases in terms of policy prescriptions. A comparison of those proposals advanced by the European social democrats with the policy preferences of the largest Latin American governments[41] makes it very clear that they agreed on precisely those crucial points on which they in turn disagreed with the U.S. government. During the first few years of the Central American crisis European social democrats seemed to be going in a direction that could satisfy the expectations placed on them by many Latin American political actors. They certainly contributed during those years to the basic Latin American objective of avoiding a situation in which the crisis could be placed in a strict East-West context. After 1982, however, a perceptible change took place in the Central American activities of European social democracy which cast severe doubts on the realism of those hopes. My concluding remarks touch on this change.

Final Considerations

The high point of European social democratic interest in the Central American crisis lasted a little more than three years. After 1982 a new period was opened during which a gradual disentanglement on the part of European social democrats was in progress. European attention was renewed with the efforts to develop a program of economic cooperation launched at the San José meeting in September 1984.[42] Such attention, however, was quite different from that during the initial period of Western European commitment. The economic cooperation was a governmental enterprise which included all governments of the European Community (EC) rather than only those under social democratic control. Social democratic forces themselves took an increasingly restrained attitude. The Spanish Socialist government, in particular, seemed constrained by an apparent desire to keep good working relations with all its former colonies in the isthmus, which brought it to a conscious effort not to "take sides" in the conflict. Little by little the Nordic socialists became the most important Western European alternatives for the Sandinista government and the revolutionary movement in El Salvador.

There are several reasons for such a shift. They have to do with changes in European politics, the activities undertaken by other governments in relation to the conflict, and the development of the Central American crisis itself. Among the most important of the first set of changes was the consolidation of Conservative rule in two important Western European countries, Germany and Great Britain, and the increasing problems of the Socialist party in France. West Germany and Great Britain were among the first European members of the Atlantic alliance to change their original policy of providing options to the Sandinista regime within the West. In that sense, at least part of the restraint exhibited after 1984 by the European social democratic governments reflected the nature itself of the multilateral exercise in which all of them participated starting that year.

The French were a good example of another interesting set of circumstances: just as their relative lack of vital interests in Central America had given them a freer hand to act in more "progressive" ways than was the case in their own former colonies, it also made them less likely to pay the price implied by opposition to the policy in their own country and on the part of the U.S. government. Complicating matters in either one of those arenas as a result of policies they might adopt in connection with a relatively secondary issue in their agenda seemed unnecessary.

This brings us to our second set of developments. Actions by both the United States government and those of Latin American countries in the immediate vicinity of the conflict were important in limiting the commitment of European social democrats. As regards U.S. actions, the displeasure of conservative U.S. thinkers with the activities of the Western European socialists in connection with the Central American crisis[43] was not a secret, even at the beginning of the Reagan administration. The administration itself gave clear signs of concern. In February 1981 Ambassador Eagleburger visited the main Western European capitals in an effort to sell the U.S. government's views on the crisis. The following year a National Security Council memorandum was leaked to the U.S. press in which the effort to change the attitudes of the Socialist International in connection with the Central American crisis was presented as one of the key priorities in the administration's Central American agenda. As the priority assigned by the Reagan administration to the subregional conflict became increasingly clear, the perception of potential costs to be paid by those forces that insisted on developing alternative policies also grew.

It is, of course, very difficult, with the information available in public sources at this point, to prove any instances of open pressure on these government or political groups or to establish clear lines of causality between their changes of behavior and U.S. displeasure. But it is difficult to deny that such displeasure, and the U.S. government's intention to correct the sources of that displeasure, were well known to the parties involved.

A more relaxed attitude on the part of Western Europe's political forces was made easier as a consequence of the actions of those Latin American governments that became identified as the "Contadora group." In a sense, the existence of the Latin American effort and the commitment of key Latin American countries to sustaining that effort made it relatively easier for the European governments to simply transform their own efforts into support for the regional initiative. And, as with many other such instances of formal support its concrete expressions were often quite limited.

As regards the evolution of the Central American crisis itself, two developments seem particularly relevant. The first was the increased Soviet support for the Nicaraguan revolution and the radicalization of the process itself. As had been the case with the Cuban revolution, many social democrats saw both as almost inevitable results of the pressure put on the revolutionary regime by the United States. But whatever its causes, the result itself, with all its implications, remained. And even as some social democrats still struggled to keep some space open for the Nicaraguans, the more open changes of other European governments significantly changed the context in which their alternative policies had to be pursued.

The attitudes of other European political forces—in this case the Christian Democratic parties of key countries such as, again, West Germany—were also particularly relevant in the context of the second Central American development: the seeming consolidation of the Duarte government in El Salvador.

But whatever the reasons for the dampening of European social democratic activities in Central America, their apparent restraint brought about a clear sobering of Latin American expectations regarding their potential role as counterweights of U.S. presence in the subregion at the political level. Such revision of previous hopes has centered on two kinds of considerations. The first, as I mentioned earlier, is the limited extent of the European economic commitment, in particular when compared with the kinds of resources that the Reagan administration has been willing to invest in support of its own policy preferences. The second is the increasingly critical tone of the evaluation that many of those social democratic parties have tended to make of the internal politics of the Nicaraguan revolution, which do not seem to take into account the national emergency created for that country by the low-intensity warfare directed from Washington. It would seem as if those European political forces were consciously or unconsciously playing into the hands of precisely one of the objectives of such strategy—to bring about an increase in Nicaragua's international isolation. Such critical tone increased with the failure of the efforts of the 1984 Rio de Janeiro meeting of the International to bring the Sandinistas and then *contra* leader Arturo Cruz to agree on terms that would guarantee the latter's participation in the Nicaraguan electoral process that same year.

Two final elements must be included in the evaluation of the European social democratic retreat. The first points to the fact that the Central American revolutionary forces still enjoy the sympathy of important segments of European social democratic constituencies, as the reception given to the Nicaraguan president and vice-president during their European tours amply shows. As a result, even if those constituencies limit their support of the Sandinista revolution, they still cannot publicly support the policies pursued by the Reagan administration. This in turn is important for the forces within the United States that oppose those policies: they can point to European disagreements as one proof of their mistaken nature. In a sense, we seem to face a "juego a cuatro bandas" in which the support of European public opinion limits the public statements of the European governments, which in turn affects the U.S. political debate in ways that limit the U.S. administration's ability to act in accordance with its own preferences.

The second point that must be included in our evaluation is in turn related to the changing political circumstances of key South American countries where four factors may help to bring a renewed European social democratic presence to those countries. First, there is a stronger tradition of both social democratic and European presence in South America than in the isthmus. Second, European economic and other interests involved in that part of the world are considerably more important. Third, significant sectors of those countries' Left have tended to move in an increasingly social democratic direction. Finally, the United States seems to be willing to tolerate a greater degree of "heterodox" behavior there than seems to be the case in what it clearly still considers its own sphere of influence.

Part Two of the History of the Renewed Presence of European Social Democracy in Latin America, in sum, may have to be written from a Southern Cone perspective, now that Part One seems to have ended on a clearly anticlimactic note. Perhaps the story will include more adventurous turns in that second installment.

NOTES

1. William D. Rogers, "U.S. Behavior and European Apprehensions," in Joseph Cirincione, ed., *Central America and the Western Alliance* (New York: Holmes & Meier, 1985).

2. Carlos Rico F., "Common Concerns and National Interests: The Contadora Experience and the Prospects for Collective Security Arrangements in the Western Hemisphere." Paper prepared for the World Peace Foundation's Project on Collective Security in the Western Hemisphere, 1987.

3. Laurence Whitehead, "Debt, Diversification and Dependency: Latin America's International Political Relations," in Kevin Middlebrook and Carlos Rico F., eds., *The United States and Latin America in the 1980's: Contending Perspectives on a Decade of Crisis* (Pittsburgh: Pittsburgh University Press, 1986).

4. G.D.H. Cole, *Historia del Pensamiento Socialista* (México: Fondo de Cultura Económica, 1974), vol. 4, p. 273.

5. Ibid.

6. Karl-Ludwig Günsche and K. Lantermann, *Historia de la Internacional Socialista* (México: Nueva Imagen, 1979), pp. 190-191. Quoted in Felicity Williams, *La Internacional Socialista y America Latina* (México: Universidad Autónoma Metropolitana Azcapotzalco, 1984), p. 106.

7. Williams, p. 90.

8. Michael Lowy, "Trayectoria de la Internacional Socialista en América Latina," *Cuadernos Políticos*, no. 29 (July-September 1981).
9. Williams, pp. 194-195.
10. Lowy, p. 38.
11. Jenny Pearce, ed., *The European Challenge: Europe's New Role in Latin America* (London: Latin America Bureau, 1982), p. 6.
12. As quoted in Williams, p. 125.
13. Pierre Schori, *El desafío europeo en Centroamérica* (San José: Editorial Universitaria Centroamericana, 1982), pp. 251-254.
14. *Nueva Sociedad*, no. 39 (November/December 1979), p. 12. It is interesting to note that Granada's New Jewel Movement also requested admission in the International, and that it was accepted in 1980. Also, in 1980 a request for membership presented by Nicaragua's Movimiento Democrático Nicaraguense, headed by Alfonso Robelo, was denied.
15. Laurence Whitehead, "International Aspects of Democratization," in Guillermo O'Donnell, Philippe C. Schmitter and Laurence Whitehead, eds., *Transitions from Authoritarian Rule: Comparative Perspectives* (Baltimore: The Johns Hopkins University Press, 1986), p. 10.
16. Schori, pp. 251-254.
17. A good summary of the limited economic presence of key European countries in the region is presented in Esperanza Durán: *European Interests in Latin America* (London: The Royal Institute of International Affairs, 1985). See also Sistema Económico Latinoamericano, *América Latina y la Comunidad Económica Europea: Problemas y Perspectives* (Caracas: Monte Ávila Editores, 1983).
18. Pearce, p. 7.
19. Jacqueline Roddick and Philip O'Brien, "Europe and Latin America in the Eighties," in Pearce, *The European Challenge*.
20. Willy Brandt, Bruno Kreisky, and Olof Palme, *La Alternativa socialdemócrata* (Barcelona: Blume, 1977), p. 128.
21. Karel E. Vosskühler, "The EEC and the USA: Differing Politico-Economic Approaches," in Christopher Stevens, ed., *EEC and the Third World: A Survey*, vol 3: *The Atlantic Rift* (New York: Holmes & Meier, 1983).
22. Statements the secretary general of the organization, B. Carlsson, made on September 13 and 21, 1978, reproduced in *Socialist Affairs*, no. 6 (1978), p. 171. Quoted in Williams, pp. 251, 252.
23. Perhaps the most prominent case was that of Hector Oqueli, member of the Salvadoran MNR, who in the late seventies became a member of the secretariat in charge of Latin American affairs. Mr. Oqueli is at present a prominent figure in El Salvador's Democratic Revolutionary Front, which along with the Farabundo Martí National Liberation Front constitutes part of the armed opposition in that country: FDR-FMLN.
24. Walter LaFeber, "The Reagan Administration and Revolutions in Central America," in *Political Science Quarterly* (Spring 1984), p. 10.
25. Víctor Bulmer-Thomas, "Relaciones Económicas Entre Centroamérica y Europa Occidental," *Cuadernos Semestrales de los Estados Unidos: perspectiva latinoamericana*, no.18 (1985).
26. Frederick Tanner, "Un nuevo aspecto en la solución del conflicto en América Central: Europa y Contadora," *Cuadernos Semestrales de los Estados Unidos: perspectiva latinoamericana*, no. 18, (1985).
27. Ibid.
28. Schori, pp. 251-254.

29. Schori, p. 14.
30. See, for example, Fernando Morán, "Europe's Role in Central America: A Spanish Socialist View," in Andrew J. Pierre, ed., *Third World Instability: Central America as a European American Issue* (New York: Council on Foreign Relations, 1985).
31. Schori, pp. 255-257.
32. Ibid., p. 28.
33. Ibid., p. 37.
34. Ibid., p. 43.
35. Ibid., p. 94-95.
36. Ibid., p. 210.
37. See, for example, the text of a document prepared under the auspices of German and Dutch social democrats which was to be endorsed by most European social democratic parliamentarians: *The Central American Crisis: A European Response* (Amsterdam: Transnational Institute, 1984). See also the critique of the Kissinger report presented by two influential members of the British Parliament, in Stuart Holland and Donald Anderson, *Kissinger's Kingdom: A Counter Report on Central America* (London: Spokesman. 1984).
38. Holland and Anderson, p. 11.
39. Wolf Grabendorff, "Western European Perceptions of the Crisis in Central America," in Wolf Grabendorff, Heinrich W. Krumwiede and Jorg Todt, *Political Change in Central America: Internal and External Dimensions* (Boulder, Colo.: Westview Press, 1984), p. 289.
40. Wolf Grabendorff, "The Central American Crisis: Is there a Role for Western Europe?," in Joseph Cirincione, ed., *Central America and the Western Alliance* (New York: Holmes & Meier, 1985), p. 129.
41. See pp. 95–97 in this volume.
42. José Miguel Insulza, "Europa, Centroamérica y la Alianza Atlántica," *Cuadernos Semestrales de los Estados Unidos: perspectiva latinoamericana*, no. 18, (1985).
43. See, for example, Irving Kristol, "Should Europe Be Concerned About Central America?," in Pierre.

8

Spain, the United States, and NATO: Strategic Facts and Political Realities

Gregory F. Treverton

For every solution, there is a problem, General de Gaulle is supposed to have said.[1] So it is with Spain and NATO. In office, Felipe González changed his mind about NATO and managed to bring his Socialist party, the Partido Socialista Obrero Español (PSOE), with him; he capped that turnabout with a surprisingly large victory for staying in NATO in a 1986 referendum that had looked like a good tactic for gracefully exiting NATO but a poor one for staying in. Fifty-three percent of those Spaniards who voted opted to remain in NATO. (The extent of the achievement is suggested by polls three years before, which indicated that 43 percent of those polled opposed staying in and only 13 percent favored it.)

Now the problem: the "yes" vote González won was achieved at the price of the three conditions. One, a continuation of Spain's nonnuclear status, no longer is controversial. Of the other two, however, the second (*not* joining NATO's integrated military command) raises uncertainties for the longer term, while the third ("a progressive reduction in the U.S. military presence in Spain") is an immediate issue.

NATO and the EEC

The stories of Spain's membership in both NATO and the European Community (EC) are well known and hardly need rehearsing here. The first point is that from the rebirth of Spanish democracy in 1977, the EC and NATO issues were intertwined. They were linked both in substance, as twin symbols of Spain rejoining the democratic West, and tactically, with Spanish governments at various times using

NATO membership to prod its would-be Common Market partners and EC entry to shore up domestic support for NATO.

Second, from the start the EC question was more pressing. Spain first applied for Community membership in June 1977, within weeks of its first democratic elections since the 1930s. Membership was widely popular across the political spectrum. In the first flush of democratization, the general eagerness to join the democracies overshadowed more specific worries about what membership might mean for Spanish industrial and agricultural producers. Spain's application followed those of Greece (June 1975) and Portugal (March 1977), but it was clear from the start that Spain would be the hardest for the Community to digest, given its size, industrial output, and agricultural products. It suffices to sketch three phases of the process, and the different links to the NATO issue in each.[2]

In the first several years after Spain's application, the "high politics" of reinforcing Spain's transition to democracy seemed to dominate the reactions of its would-be partners. Opposition from French and Italian agricultural producers, which would have to compete with Spanish producers, was predictable, as was the prospect that domestic politics would give those interests influence out of proportion to their numbers, especially with the conservative governments then in power in Paris and Rome.

Nevertheless, those obstacles appeared to on the way to being overcome, first in Italy and later, more reluctantly, in France under Valéry Giscard d'Estaing. In December 1978 France agreed to give unanimous approval to the EC Commission's "Opinion on Spain's Application for Membership." That opinion outlined the practical problems of Spanish accession but emphasized the political desirability of incorporating democratic Spain into Europe.[3] During this hopeful period in the EC negotiations, the NATO question was in the background. Activities of the government and of NATO supporters outside government were limited to trying to inform themselves—and such of their public as was interested—about what NATO was and might mean for Spain.

The center-right government of the Unión del Centro Democrático (UCD) had declared its general support for NATO membership as early as autumn 1978, but its overriding imperative at this point was putting together a domestic political compact that would permit it to carry out the needed economic austerity program. In the Pact of Moncloa of October 1977 the Left—including both PSOE and the Partido Comunista Español (PCE)—agreed to such a program. In the process the parties implicitly agreed to hold to the status quo in foreign policy: the Left would not campaign against the

American bases in Spain if the government would not push the NATO issue.

A second phase began abruptly in June 1980. Giscard, reversing his position, called for a "freeze" in Spain's application process until the Community had adjusted so as to make Spanish membership harmless to French interests. His decision seems to have been motivated by domestic politics as he sought to shore up his flanks in anticipation of the 1981 presidential elections.

The French *non* changed the Spanish approach to the EC and NATO issues. Spain's foreign minister, Marcelino Oreja, announced to a surprised public in June 1980 that the government intended to take Spain into NATO in the near future, although he did condition entry on two "guarantees...that the process of Spain's integration into the EC will continue, and that Hispano-British negotiation is underway and the transfer of sovereignty over Gibraltar to Spain is approaching a solution."[4] Both then and two years later when Spain did join NATO the primary purpose seems to have been more tactical—putting pressure on France to move forward with the EC negotiations—than any overriding desire to join the alliance. As UCD secretary for foreign affairs, Javier Rupérez, put it: "France cannot be permitted to be the last bastion against the amplification of the EEC."[5]

Between 1980 and 1982 there intervened the attempted military coup of February 1981, thus giving the government yet another reason to take Spain into NATO. Yet the tactical nature of the government's action was suggested by its statement in the autumn of 1980 that NATO membership should not be pursued at the cost of unduly upsetting the PSOE, which still opposed membership.[6] Clearly, joining NATO was not worth a domestic fight. When membership came in June 1982, it was almost an act of desperation by a failing government that was unable to end the impasse in the EC negotiations and was searching for surrogates for a foreign policy it did not really have.

By the time of the Spanish election in October 1982, EC membership no longer fired the imaginations of Spaniards as it once had. The wrangle over membership already had been a long one and was about to become longer still as the Community entered its two-year fight over the budget. Spanish businessmen worried that they would not be able to compete in the EC. Yet if enthusiasm had waned, there remained a broad base of support for EC membership in Spain, and the issue was not a major one in the October elections.

Those elections were a stunning—though not surprising—victory for the PSOE and Felipe González. The UCD was never quite able to shed its Franco origins—its creator, Adolfo Suárez, himself had been a rising technocrat in the old regime. Moreover, the challenges confronting it were daunting: dealing with the economy and with terrorism in the Basque country while implanting democratic institutions throughout Spain. It always was more an electoral convenience than a real party, and when Suárez resigned in frustration in January 1981, it was the beginning of the end.

Under González, the EC-NATO connection moved from a second to a third phase. Though NATO membership was for him a *fait accompli*, and one to which his party was opposed to boot, he, too, seems to have tried to use that *fait* to put pressure on the EC negotiations. On a visit to Bonn in May 1983 he expressed "comprehension of and solidarity with" the NATO decision to deploy 572 cruise and Pershing nuclear missiles in Europe depending on the outcome of the Geneva arms control negotiations.[7] His statement provoked anger within the party and large protests outside it. On his return to Madrid, however, González is reported to have suggested that the wording of the proposed referendum on NATO could depend on how the EC negotiations progressed.[8]

González himself seems to have changed his mind about NATO soon after he came to power, perhaps even before. He did so not because of any fresh analysis of Spain's strategic position, but rather because of "the power of events and of facts," as a senior foreign ministry official put it to me in June 1985. The timing of his public turnaround seems to have been dictated by the pace of the EC negotiations and by the need to keep his party with him. He announced the change in his state-of-the-nation speech in October 1984, on the eve of PSOE's thirtieth party congress.

The first two items of his ten-point program—later referred to by his followers, somewhat grandly, as the "decalogue"—were remaining in NATO but staying aloof from the integrated military command.[9] Other important particulars also foreshadowed the later referendum campaign: commitments to reduce the U.S. military presence in Spain, to keep Spain denuclearized, to work toward regaining sovereignty over Gibraltar, and to increase military cooperation with other nations of Western Europe.

In this third phase, the EC-NATO link worked in both directions: NATO membership was a lever on the EC negotiations, and González plainly hoped that Common Market entry would mute domestic opposition to NATO. The timing of the NATO referendum thus was conditioned on when Spain joined the EC, and that, of course, continued to put pressure on Spain's would-be EC partners to make good their commitment on Spanish entry. In these circumstances, the logjam finally broke. Both Spain and the EC made concessions in the final negotiations, and Spain, with Portugal, joined the Community in January 1986.

The American Connection

Like the issue of EC membership, the bilateral U.S.-Spanish defense relationship bore on the question of NATO membership. It still does. When Spain was rebuffed in its efforts to join both the EC and NATO, despite American sponsorship of the latter, Franco's attention then turned to the bilateral relationship with the United States. He found the Eisenhower administration seeking European real estate on which to base its nuclear bombers (and later submarines) that yet lacked range enough to reach Soviet targets from the continental United States. Washington and Madrid accordingly agreed, in September 1953, to a bilateral defense agreement providing for U.S. use of Spanish bases in exchange for economic assistance. More important to Franco, perhaps, was the political symbolism; he called the agreements the "most important element in our contemporary foreign policy."[10]

This bilateral relationship has implicated the United States in the Franco legacy in at least two ways. First, it contributed to the feeling, fair enough, that the United States helped sustain the Franco regime. That sentiment spreads across the political spectrum short only of the unreconstructed Right. Conservative foreign minister Pérez Llorca said in 1981 that the bilateral relationship was "clearly precarious and unsatisfactory . . . tantamount to satellization."[11] As Socialist leader González put it more sharply: "America helped Europe to free itself from fascism, and it not only did not help Spain but condemned it to dictatorship for many more years...We have little for which to thank the United States, the last country with which we were at war."[12]

A second strand of sentiment hangs over the current events in a still more direct way. Given Franco's desperation, it was—and still is—easy for Spaniards to feel that Spain paid, and still may pay, too high a price for its link to the United States. That feeling is summed up by a story, perhaps true, about a Franco communication to his negotiators in Washington during a difficult period in the negotiations. "Bargain hard," he is said to have written, "and if you come up with nothing, sign it."

The sense that Spain may have been had is reinforced when

earlier nuclear arrangements, like those under the first Spanish-American treaty, are judged by light of the nuclear anxieties of the 1980s. That is true despite the fact that under the 1976 version of the treaty the United States withdrew all its nuclear missile-carrying submarines from Rota by mid-1979 and pledged not to "store nuclear weapons or their components on Spanish soil."[13] Spanish commentators have focused on the secret annexes to the agreements setting out when the United States could conduct operations from the bases. By current lights, those provisions seem vague in descriptions both of possible threats and of the areas from whence they might emanate. The fact that the bases were put on alert during crises over Cuba or in the Middle East, even though Spain was not directly involved, now looks like the treaty endangered Spain more than it protected it.[14]

In 1976, after the death of Franco, the United States sought to draw Spain further into Western military arrangements, and the bilateral agreement was converted into a Treaty of Friendship and Cooperation, which entered into force in September 1976.[15] That provided for a United States-Spanish Council explicitly intended to serve as a bridge to ultimate Spanish membership in NATO. A new executive agreement on the use of bases in Spain was reached in July 1982, just after Spain joined NATO. Under it the United States agreed to provide over $400 million annually, almost all, however, in the form of credits for Foreign Military Sales (FMS).

Yet, before that new agreement could enter force González was elected and froze Spain's integration into the NATO military structure. Madrid and Washington negotiated a protocol to the July agreement, in which Spain made clear that the agreement did not prejudice the choice about full military integration with NATO, and the agreement entered force in May 1983. González supported the agreement once the protocol had been agreed, and it easily passed the Socialist-controlled Cortes. The agreement is to last five years—thus the immediacy of the base issue.

Under the agreement the United States has access to four main bases—the Rota Naval Base (100 kilometers northwest of Gibraltar) and air bases at Torrejón (near Madrid), Zaragoza, and Morón—plus a number of smaller facilities, especially military communications installations. Some 12,000 Americans, mostly Air Force, are stationed in Spain. Rota provides a staging point for airborne antisubmarine warfare, and it is also the terminal for the U.S. Defense Communications System, linked to other facilities in Spain, Italy, and Greece and to the Sixth Fleet. Torrejón is home base for a tactical fighter wing that rotates planes through Aviano, Italy and Incirlik,

Turkey. Its location near Madrid, a positive symbol for Franco, now makes it, unhappily, a noise hazard and block to growth in Madrid's suburbs. Zaragoza is used for fighter training, and Morón is a backup base.

In military terms, the bases are useful but probably not vital. If they were lost to the United States, their individual missions could be compensated for, though with some difficulty and increased cost. At least they could be substituted for if the United States retained access to other bases in the area, especially those in the Azores and in Italy. One of the indirect costs of losing Spanish bases would be an increase in U.S. dependence on those bases in other countries.

The bases are less valuable to the United States than they might otherwise be because U.S. forces are deeply constrained in using them for purposes beyond NATO. In 1973, even under Franco, Spain denied Washington permission to trans-ship arms through Spain to Israel, and in 1979 the UCD government denied the United States permission to refuel in Spain F-15s bound for Saudi Arabia during the Iranian crisis. The 1982 agreement is explicit that prior permission for such uses have to be obtained from relevant Spanish authorities.[16] Even if Spain is generally forthcoming in granting such permission—as it has been in recent years—the rub for the United States is planning for a crisis. Whatever the state of peacetime cooperation, it is hard to believe that a Spanish government of any stripe will be less cautious in a crisis than those in the past have been. And so the United States will be unable to count on the bases for purposes outside NATO, especially for sensitive operations in the region where they are most likely to be required—in the Middle East and the Persian Gulf.

The referendum result, and the parallel PSOE initiative to reduce the number of U.S. troops in Spain, is another source of uncertainty. Before the referendum, González indicated on a number of occasions that Spain would continue the bilateral agreement even if the country withdrew entirely from NATO. Economic aid was a powerful original motivation on the Spanish side for the agreements in the first place, and the agreements have been relatively lucrative for Spain, though Spaniards debate how valuable they have been. In them the United States pledged to provide "defense support...in the highest amounts, the most favorable terms and the wide variety of forms" possible. During 1951-1974, the United States provided about $4 billion in aid to Spain under the agreements, about evenly divided between economic and military assistance.[17]

The Military Question: External and Internal

On paper, the Spanish military looks impressive. Its armed forces of 330,000 ranks sixth in NATO, after the United States, Turkey, France, the Federal Republic of Germany, and Italy, and just ahead of Britain; and its reservists, over a million strong, rank second only to the United States.[18] Yet, while some of Spain's military capabilities are indeed impressive, much of its hardware is a generation behind that of the principal NATO nations. In 1984, defense spending amounted only to about 10 percent of the government budget and only about 2 percent of GDP, although these figures exclude the civil guard and retirement pay. And its effectiveness, especially beyond Spain's borders, is further limited by the legacy of its traditional missions—territorial defense and internal security. Part of the reason for current reform efforts is to make the Spanish military a more effective fighting force.

The army accounts for three-fourths (240,000) of Spain's military manpower; that size is to be trimmed to 195,000. Conscripts—who formally serve for fifteen months, to be reduced to twelve, but who usually in fact have served thirteen months or less—make up 170,000 of the army.[19] The army has been organized around nine military regions, to be reduced to six, and it has virtually no capability to project power into Central Europe (the "Blue Division" that fought on the central front in World War II was furnished logistics by Germany). Of its 750-odd tanks, two-thirds are venerable U.S. M-47s and M-48s; the remainder are French AMX-30s.[20] Some 40,000 troops are deployed outside continental Spain—19,000 in Ceuta and Melilla, 16,000 in the Canary Islands, and 5,800 in the Balearic Islands.

The navy, 57,000 strong, has thirty-five major combatants—eleven destroyers, eleven frigates, four corvettes, eight submarines and a World War II-vintage aircraft carrier, with nine Harrier jets or twenty-four helicopters. It also has a wide variety of minesweeping, antisubmarine, coastal patrol, and support craft, as well as 12,000 marines and numbers of landing craft. Modernization programs contemplated for the mid-1980s, in addition to replacing Spain's aircraft carrier with one built mostly in Spain and launched in 1982, will give it several more frigates, corvettes, and submarines. In addition, the Spanish merchant marine consists of nearly 500 registered ships, the fifth largest in Western Europe.[21]

The air force is the most "professional" service in having the smallest proportion of conscripts. It is designed to provide tactical support to ground and naval units, and it has only limited means to project power or transport forces over long distances. Its inventory of 215 combat aircraft consists of U.S. F-4s and F-5s, and French Mirage IIIs and F-1s; seventy-two U.S. F-18s are on order, although that program has been the subject of controversy between Madrid and Washington. In 1977 Spain inaugurated its *Combate Grande* program to upgrade its air defenses, particularly against possible threats from the south.

All of the Spanish services have too many officers and officers that are too old. In that regard, they continue to resemble Latin American armies more than their counterparts in northern Europe. For example, in 1977 there were as many officers in the army as noncommissioned officers, and one officer for every six or seven conscripts.[22] There were 340 generals, and many of those were over seventy years old. Reducing the size of the officer corps has thus been a critical—and sensitive—element of military reform. By 1984 the number of army generals had been reduced to about 200, but there were still as many officers as noncommissioned officers in the service.[23]

Given its top-heaviness and the emphasis on territorial defense, it is no surprise that the Spanish military has spent a much larger fraction of its budget on personnel costs than other European forces. In this respect, also, it has resembled Latin American militaries more than European. In 1968 the Spanish army spent 82 percent of its budget on personnel, and even in 1976-1978, the entire Spanish armed forces still spent almost 62 percent of its allocations on personnel.[24] For comparison, the percentages for the Federal Republic of Germany, Belgium, France, Britain, and Italy were, respectively, 43, 50, 35, 40, and 34.

The defense programming law that went into effect in 1983—written by the services under the UCD government but adopted in broad outline by the PSOE administration—aims to redress that imbalance. Under it, equipment budgets will increase annually by a minimum of 4.43 percent in real terms, faster than overall budget growth, planned for an annual average of 2.5 percent.[25] The emphasis in that procurement program is on air and naval forces—a new naval combat group, new generations of aircraft for combat, transport, and maritime patrol, and air defense—with new battle tanks for the army.

The distribution of the military budget among the services has changed dramatically in the last decade. As late as 1977 the army still took over half the total budget, with the other two services sharing the remainder. By 1979, however, the army share had been reduced to 38 percent, with the navy taking thirty-five and the air force 26 percent.[26] The prospect of further change, like the need to reduce the numbers of officers, hangs over the debate within the military about future Spanish security arrangements. It has not been lost on army officers that more professionalism—and a closer approach to NATO—could mean fewer of their kind and even greater emphasis on the air and naval missions that Spain could carry out.

The reasons for reform, however, have more to do with internal arrangements—the future of Spanish democracy—than with external threats. For most of the last half century, and indeed for most of Spanish history, the Spanish military, more precisely the army, has been a principal actor—some might say the principal actor—in Spanish politics. The army was the service most loyal to Franco and most involved in fighting on his behalf during the civil war. After 1939 the army in effect became the regime, with retired officers placed in key sectors of national life. More recent events, especially the abortive 1981 coup attempt, underscore that a direct role by the military in politics is no mere historical footnote.

All militaries are institutions apart. Yet a "bunker" mentality was especially pronounced in the Spanish military before 1977, forged in the crucible of civil war and charged with upholding the systems. The military shopped in its own stores; it educated its children in military schools. By one account, over 50 percent of the officers married daughters of fellow officers.[27] No doubt, part of the emphasis on the separateness of the institution was defensive: after all, when fighting foreigners (as opposed to each other) the military's recent record was not impressive.

Yet, in the process of insulating the military as an institution and identifying it with the Franco regime, the values and practices of the military became equated with those of Spain. The first UCD government sought to avoid a purge of the officer corps, and instead tried to promote progressive officers more rapidly. That brought Suárez and his defense minister, General Gutiérrez Mellado, into collision with the fixed promotion system that was central to the military as an institution. The fight over promotions ranked with the legalization of the PCE in the military's litany of grievances against the government.

Thus, the reform process after 1977 had two objectives: to professionalize the military as a fighting force and, even more important, to break the link between the military as an institution and politics, thereby removing the officer corps from national politics. There have been two major elements to the reform process. The first, army modernization (META in its Spanish acronym), was drawn up by the army chiefs of staff in the early 1980s but put into effect by the PSOE government. The other, more sweeping, was announced by the

González government in 1983 and enacted into law in 1984.

In its most recent formulation, META will reduce the size of the army by about 90,000 by 1990, to 150,000; the officer corps (including noncommissioned officers) will be reduced by about one-quarter, from 41,000 in 1984 to 35,000, with the prospect of a further reduction later; a flexible promotion system, substituting seniority for merit, is to be introduced; and the reduction in the conscription period from fifteen to twelve months will be put into effect. After the cut in the officer corps, META's most significant feature is the reduction in military regions from nine to six, with the accompanying abolition of the nine territorial operational defense (DOT) brigades, whose primary mission was internal security and which were stretched too thinly and had poor morale.

The army will be reorganized into a five-division force, with eleven brigades, plus three independent brigades. Each of the six regions will deploy a division or at least several brigades, and major units will be moved out of cities—the previous deployments were another legacy of the internal security mission. Deployments in the Canary and Balearic Islands and in Ceuta and Melilla will remain basically unchanged.

The 1984 defense law is intended to establish clearly the principle of civilian control. Until 1977 Spain had three separate ministries for the services, each headed by a general or admiral. There was a joint staff but one with virtually no power and almost no function. In 1977 the civilian government set up a single defense ministry—whose first two ministers were, however, generals—and established a joint chiefs of staff (JUJEM) to formulate a plan for defense structure. JUJEM took decisions unanimously, and the chairman had no independent authority.

The 1984 law buttresses the position of the defense minister. The service chiefs exercise their commands "under the authority of" the minister, and the law carefully distinguishes between the "authority" of the government and the "command" responsibilities of generals. In place of JUJEM, the law creates a chief of defense staff (JEMAD), with powers much greater than the chairman of JUJEM. JEMAD is the "principal collaborator of the Minister, to whom he is responsible for the planning and execution of the operational aspects of military policy."[28]

Looking to the Future

The cluster of issues—Spain's relations to the United States and to NATO, and its military reform—have at least as much to do with domestic politics as foreign policy. So, too, the perspective of Spain's partners in NATO is more political than military: how to ensure the continuity of democracy in Spain and the firm membership of that country among the world's industrial democracies. This brief survey of specific questions can provide no more than pointers for thinking about the future.

American Bases

The current agreement expires in May 1988. For his part, González is under pressure to make good on his earlier promises; he argues, moreover, that Spain, as a full member of the democratic West, ought to reduce its dependence on foreign forces.[29] By contrast, for the United States, maintenance of the U.S. bases is a test of Spain's willingness to play a role in alliance defense, all the more so since Spain remains outside the integrated military command. Behind that U.S. position is the fear that even a limited withdrawal from Spanish bases could provoke calls for similar withdrawals elsewhere—Greece, for example.

The positions of the two sides suggest little room for compromise, but the history of the bases, even under Socialist government in Spain, seems to belie the prospect of dramatic change. Still, there is the risk that domestic politics could drive González to harder policies than he might prefer. For Spain, the issues of NATO and the U.S. connection have been, even more so than is the case for most "foreign policy" issues in most countries, dominated by their domestic face. As a senior foreign policy adviser to the government said to me in June 1985: "NATO has been a domestic matter."

Threats and Interests

The base issue raises the broader question of how Spain defines its external interests—a question that was suppressed by the isolation of the Franco period. For an outsider, the discussion of these issues remains frustratingly ill-focused. For instance, when Spaniards talk of external threats, that discussion usually is vague but the direction is always south. One senior foreign ministry official put it to me in the following way, only half-jokingly: Both nations and their militaries need threats; for Spain, the Soviet Union is too far away, and Portugal is no longer credible as a threat; but the south is "perfect, just the right size."

It is hard to know what to make of such statements. When pressed about "south," Spaniards usually seem to mean the North African cities of Ceuta and Melilla—an issue in the NATO debate when it became clear that NATO would not extend to them. Certainly, there is some threat to those enclaves, but that derives more from the fact that they are anomalies in the latter part of the twentieth century than from any more general threat that might engulf them on its way to mainland Spain. Similarly, the Canary Islands, a thousand kilometers from the mainland, have seen occasional outbreaks of violence in the past. However, the threat to the Canaries is more internal—separatists, perhaps seeking external aid—than classic external aggression. It is worth noting that in the past the Spanish military, at least, did not seem to take such threats seriously enough to redeploy forces away from territorial defense and internal security. Even those units designed for the defense of borders, like the armored division, were based far from frontiers and close to major population centers.

By the same token, once freed from the isolation of the Franco period, Spanish governments have cast about for a broader, more independent foreign policy. They have, in particular, emphasized Spain's vocation in both the Latin America and the Arab worlds. Adolfo Suárez reportedly was not eager to push forward with NATO membership lest doing so damage Spain's links to Arab and Latin American states. He declared in 1978 that NATO membership did not figure among his "fourteen priorities." For similar reasons, Spain refrained from recognizing Israel, and received Palestine Liberation Organization leader Yasir Arafat, even under a UCD government. The PSOE government sought to underscore the new renewed Spanish interest in Latin America by creating a special institute for affairs with the region.

These aspirations to a wider role no doubt are real. They reflect the fact that democratic Spain has broader options, and they are also part of the search for a foreign policy that is both commensurate with Spain's new status and that will command broad political support. As Spain looks to the future, however, two questions are worth bearing in mind.

One is how much Spain's efforts in the Arab world and Latin America will matter in concrete—as opposed to domestic political—terms. In 1981 the EC nations took over 40 percent of Spain's exports and provided, oil aside, nearly half its imports. The United States took 7 percent of Spain's exports and provided 13 percent of its imports.[30] By contrast, Spain's trade with Latin America accounted for less than 10 percent of both exports and imports, and trade with the non-oil-producing countries of the Arab world was only a fraction of that figure.

There remains of course the oil link. In 1981 the oil-producing countries, mostly in the Middle East and the Gulf, provided 30.1 percent of Spain's imports and took 14.5 percent of its exports, figures that were up from 21.7 and 10.5 percent, respectively, in 1975. And for certain key exports Spain finds markets in new places. For example, like other nations at a middle level of industrialization, Spain is bound to feel that its technology is more appropriate for the developing world than that of the most industrialized nations. Spanish exports to both the Arab world and Latin America have been growing gradually as a portion of total exports. But some perspective is worthwhile. In 1985 Spain still sold more to North Africa than to Latin America; both France and West Germany had larger economic interests in Latin America than did Spain.

The other issue is how much these broader aspirations need influence central choices about relations with Europe, the EC, and NATO. Reportedly, during its EC negotiations, Spain sought, but failed, to include some language hinting that the Latin American states might receive EC preferences similar to those given to former colonies under the Lomé convention. Spain sustained close commercial relations with Castro's Cuba even during the Franco period. Or while Suárez expressed the fear that NATO membership might complicate Spain's relations in the Third World, UCD Foreign Minister Pérez Llorca expressed just the opposite view: "I have found in the Arab countries . . . an interest in knowing that they have a friend in NATO and a country which has traditionally listened to them sensitively. . . . Of course the same applies to the Latin American countries."[31] It seems hard to choose between these two views in substance, on the assumption that with any form of link to NATO Spain would be careful to avoid actions to which specific Arab nations objected.

Gibraltar, Ceuta, and Melilla

These specific questions, quiet now, remain uncertainties. Suffice it to flag them here. In staying in NATO, González adopted the logic of his conservative predecessors—that Spain would have more leverage over the Gibraltar issue *inside* the alliance than outside. Yet so long as Spain remains outside the integrated military structure, the Gibraltar issue will not be closed. The domestic passions it arouses could reawaken, putting governments under pressure to take actions they might prefer to avoid with their EC partners, especially Britain, or calling into question continued membership in NATO.

Outside Spain (and, no doubt, Morocco) only geography buffs

have even heard of Ceuta and Melilla, but inside Spain the issue is alive—and connected to both the U.S. link and to NATO. Even Spaniards who support NATO reiterate how important it is to find some formula to provide at least a fig leaf of cover for the enclaves under NATO. These same supporters of NATO are deeply suspicious of the role of the United States, some taking it as a given that Washington had supported Morocco's 1975 Green March into the Spanish Sahara, even to the point of providing logistical support.

Imagine if volatile events in North Africa put pressure on NATO and the Spanish-U.S. relationship. Any of a dozen scenarios can be imagined. Suppose, for example, that a change of government in Morocco brought to power a nationalist regime bent on taking Ceuta and Melilla. The exclusion of the enclaves from the NATO area might then become a powerful domestic argument against remaining in the alliance, all the more so if it appeared that the United States was more interested in its relations with the new regime than with Spanish concerns over the cities.

Half in, Half out

In strictly military terms, it does not matter much to NATO if Spain maintains its current ambivalence. Spain will continue to be reckoned as a political part of the West and, in any but the most dramatic terms of domestic politics, will be counted as an ally, formal or informal, as well. Even in the unlikely event that Spain chose to fully integrate itself in NATO's military command, that would be only a marginal advantage to NATO, at least for the foreseeable future (and it would be politically inconvenient with regard to Portugal). It would improve NATO's air defense, especially from the south, and it could buttress the alliance's naval capabilities, especially in the approaches to the Mediterranean. Over the longer term, and if suitable basing arrangements could be made, Spanish mobile forces might be available for reinforcement of the southern flank or, less probably, of the central front.[32] Yet these latter possibilities would presuppose a sustained improvement in Spanish forces; thus, they are a distant prospect.

What NATO most needs from Spain—the bases—it gets through the bilateral arrangements with the United States. (Interestingly, Spanish bases and forces are becoming *more* important if some analysts are correct that recent trends—in Soviet military doctrine and in antinuclear sentiment in NATO—make the prospect of a major conventional war in Europe more thinkable than before.[33] Whether Spaniards would like that development is another question!

And it is worth remembering that some of the allies fought World War II without Spain.) Even in the unlikely event that the United States lost all access to Spanish bases, that would be an inconvenience but not a disaster, provided bases in the Azores continued to be available and provided air bases in Sicily (or elsewhere) could be expanded.

From NATO's perspective the political symbolism is at least as important as the military calculations. Certainly, once Spain had joined NATO, it would have been a blow to the alliance had it left. Spain's current status is awkward, for it leaves Spanish diplomats and officers quite literally half in and half out of NATO. If Spain moves, as is likely, to NATO *à la* France, that would be no disaster, but the alliance would worry that it would abet tendencies elsewhere—again, Greece in particular—to think of special statuses. It would be one more step in a direction NATO already is taking—toward a two-tier alliance.

Domestic Politics and Foreign Policy

For Spain, too, the implications of "foreign policy" choices are more political than military. The internal debate over foreign policy is likely to remain vague. After all, the country has no obvious external enemies; its twentieth-century history of neutrality has reinforced what geography suggested. Moreover, as an experienced Spanish diplomat pointed out, Spain came of age on strategic matters in the late 1970s and early 1980s when passions on the nuclear issue were high and when the reliability of the United States was in question. That is also bound to give the debate over NATO, and foreign policy more generally, a different flavor from that of discussion in the other European countries that joined NATO when the cold war was real and the alliance a thing of necessity.

In these circumstances, the domestic debate will throw up a variety of initiatives, not all of them easily compatible. The EC will, bad accidents aside, remain more acceptable than NATO, just as identification with "Europe" will tug more on Spanish emotions than the U.S. connnection. Out of power, Spanish socialists were tempted by some "European" defense entity and were frustrated when their fellow European socialists kept telling them that there was such a grouping—and its name was NATO. If the West European Union (WEU) or some other European grouping were to amount to something, it would no doubt be attractive to Spain—either as a way to make NATO more acceptable or, depending on circumstances, as a partial substitute.

Finally, developments in foreign and security policy will also bear on domestic politics in another way. The battle for the soul of Spain's armed forces is far from over. Civilian politicians have looked to NATO membership as an incentive, one the army will find difficult to resist, to professionalize the army and remove it from politics. Clearly, the success of those endeavors will depend mostly on internal events in Spain—in particular, the military's perception of the competence of Spain's civilian leaders in dealing with terrorism and the regional question. But if efforts to integrate Spain firmly into Western institutions, including NATO, failed, or if it looked like Spain was getting too little return, the resistance of the Spanish army to move too far away from its traditional roles might increase, thus endangering Spain's political transition.

Notes

1. This article draws on, and updates, my *Spain: Domestic Politics and Security Policy*, Adelphi paper 204 (London: IISS, Spring 1986).

2. Paul Preston and Denis Smyth, *Spain, the EEC and NATO*, Chatham House Papers 22 (London, 1984), is slightly quirky and belies its title by not treating the NATO issue in any depth. But its discussion of the EC negotiations is useful. See, especially, pp. 4-16 and 66-68.

3. Commission of the EC, "Opinion on Spain's Application for Membership," Supplement 9/78, *Bulletin of the European Communities*.

4. Quoted in *El País*, June 15, 1980.

5. Cited in Preston and Smyth, p. 72.

6. Ibid.

7. *Cambio 16*, May 16 and June 27, 1983.

8. *International Herald Tribune*, June 13 and 30, 1983.

9. See "Spain and NATO: Problems of Military Integration," *International Defense Review* 1 (1985), p. 24.

10. Angel Viñas, "Perspectiva crítica sobre los acuerdos España-EE.UU," in *España. ¿qué defensa?*, (Madrid:Instituto de Cuestiones Internacionales 1981), p. 204.

11. *La Vanguardia* (Barcelona), September 1, 1981, as reported by FBIS, vol. 3, no. 178, September 14, 1981.

12. *Ya* (Madrid), November 1, 1981, as reported by FBIS, vol. 8, no. 221, November 17, 1981.

13. "Supplementary Agreement on Facilities, Treaty on Friendship and Cooperation (1976)," in *United States Treaties and Other International Agreements* 27 (Washington, 1977), pp. 3034-3035.

14. See, for example, Viñas, p. 206ff.

15. *U.S. Senate. Treaty of Friendship and Cooperation with Spain*, 94th Congress, 2nd Session (February 18, 1976). For fuller references and details, see Congressional Research Service, "United States Military Installations in Spain," Report No. 84-149 F (Washington, September 7, 1984).

16. *Agreement on Friendship, Defense and Cooperation between the United States of America and the Kingdom of Spain*, July 2, 1982, cited in Congressional Research Service, p. 12.

SPAIN, THE UNITED STATES, AND NATO   139

17. Vicenc Fisas, *El poder militar en España* (Barcelona: Editorial Laia, 1979), pp. 238-239.
18. International Institute for Strategic Studies, *The Military Balance 1984-1985* (London, 1984).
19. For statistics on the military and information about reforms, see Col. Francisco L. de Sepúlveda, "Restructuring Spain's Defense Organization," *International Defense Review* 17, no. 10 (1984), 1431-1437.
20. William L. Heiberg, *The Sixteenth Nation: Spain's Role in NATO*, Monograph Series No. 83-1 (Washington: National Defense University, 1983), p. 14ff.
21. Center for Strategic and International Studies, *The Future of U.S. Maritime Policy* (Washington, 1980), p.138.
22. See Hal Klepak, *Spain: NATO or Neutrality?* National Security Series 1/80 (Kingston, Ontario: Queen's University, 1980), pp. 39-40.
23. See *Jane's Defence Weekly*, July 28, 1984, p. 94.
24. For the earlier statistic, see Vicenc Fisas, p. 152, which though now somewhat dated is a good summary of Spanish military budgets, equipment, and industry. The later figure is from Angel Lobo and Luis Marco, "El coste económico de la defensa," in Instituto de Cuestiones Internacionales, p. 132.
25. Evamaria Loose-Weintraub, "Spain's New Defence Policy: Arms Production and Exports," SIPRI, *World Armaments and Disarmament Yearbook, 1984* (London: Taylor & Francis, 1984), p. 138.
26. Sepúlveda, p. 1435, and Klepak, pp. 31-32.
27. Cited in Preston and Smyth, p. 44.
28. See Sepúlveda, p. 1432ff.
29. See the *Wall Street Journal*, February 3, 1987.
30. These and the following statistics are from International Monetary Fund (IMF), *Direction of Trade Statistics Yearbook, 1982* (Washington: IMF, 1982).
31. As reported in *ABC* (Madrid), September 5, 1981.
32. All the possibilities are discussed in more detail in my Adelphi Paper, cited above.
33. See, for instance, Max G. Manwaring and Alan Ned Sabrosky, "Iberia's Role in NATO's Future: Strategic Reserve, Reinforcement and Redoubt," *Parameters*, 16, no. 1 (Spring 1986).

9

Spain in NATO: The Reluctant Partner

Glenn H. Snyder

This chapter has three objectives. One is to assess, in a general way, the benefits and costs to Spain, and to the alliance as a whole, of Spanish membership in NATO, under the limiting constraints specified in the referendum of March 1986. The second is to compare the posture of Spain, under these same limiting conditions, to that of certain other alliance members who may also be considered only "semialigned." Finally, sole speculation is advanced about how Spanish membership is likely to affect the movement toward European defense cooperation.

Spain in NATO: A Preliminary Balance Sheet

When Spanish voters approved Spain's continued membership in NATO, in the referendum of March 1986, they did so subject to three qualifying conditions established by the ruling Socialist party: (1) there would be no nuclear weapons on Spanish territory, (2) Spain would not participate in NATO's integrated command structure, and (3) the U.S. military presence would be reduced. Given these conditions, what are the prospective gains and costs to Spain, and to the alliance in general, from Spain's accession?

The most obvious point is that Spain will share in the benefits and costs of the formal alliance commitment and the implicit nuclear commitment of the United States. However, it is hard to see how the security benefits to Spain from these commitments will be any greater than heretofore. Prior to joining the alliance, she already enjoyed most of the benefits of U.S. nuclear deterrence simply because of her geographical position and her bilateral treaty with the

United States. Deterrence of a Soviet conventional attack on West Germany was, and is, automatically deterrence of an attack on Spain as well. Of course, the value of the U.S. nuclear deterrent must be discounted by the possible costs of supporting it. Spain has sought to minimize such cost by forbidding deployment of nuclear weapons on her territory, thus reducing her attractiveness as a nuclear target. Soviet propaganda directed to Spain has assiduously promoted the idea that deployment means devastation. However, it seems likely that the U.S. bases in Spain would be as much a magnet for nuclear strikes as nuclear weapons. In any event, by a U.S.-Spanish agreement negotiated in 1976, there have been no nuclear weapons on Spanish territory since 1979.

Aside from nuclear deterrence, the other kind of security benefit that Spain might derive from NATO membership is a greater capability for non-nuclear defense of her territory. Here again, simply the formal commitment of other European countries to defend Spain makes very little difference, since NATO forces in West Germany and France would automatically be defending Spain in the process of defending their own territory. Security gains for Spain would come from whatever Spain contributed to the overall strength and effectiveness of NATO's conventional defenses. Spain's contribution in this respect could be quite significant, but much of it would require coordination of plans with other NATO forces.

Her most valuable contribution might be simply her territory. One of NATO's major weaknesses in a conventional war is a lack of geographical depth. Given France's arms-length relationship to NATO, the alliance's combined operations and supporting facilities on the central front virtually stop at the Franco-German border. Although French territory would no doubt be available during wartime for at least some functions (including retreat!), much of the value of depth is peacetime value. Spanish territory could provide greater safety and efficiency for many facilities and functions that are now crammed into the Low Countries-West German corridor. It would provide, for example, protected rear areas for storage and stockpiling of supplies and equipment, for dispersed basing of aircraft, for training exercises, and for command and control facilities. It would also provide safe entry points for reinforcements from the United States in wartime and staging areas for their transport to the front. Location of NATO facilities in Spain would no doubt require negotiation of limited transit rights across French territory in peacetime, subject to expansion in wartime.

The ultimate value of Spanish territory could be as a "strategic redoubt" into which retreating NATO armies could regroup and recover their strength, or at least gain additional time before having to make the decision whether to go nuclear or surrender.[1] The Pyrenees are a more formidable barrier than anything a Soviet invading force would confront in northern Europe and, with proper advance preparation, could hold that force up for a significant time. Advance preparation would have to include plans for the bombing and mining of choke points and transportation routes, to be carried out, perhaps, by Spanish tactical air forces and engineers. The time thus obtained could be used to bring in reinforcements from the United States and other NATO countries, and to reorganize and resupply the retreating NATO forces. During the delay, airpower based in Spain could disrupt overstretched Soviet supply and communications systems. The longer Spain remained in NATO's hands, the longer NATO naval forces could block Soviet naval operations. The knowledge that such a strategic redoubt existed, and that NATO forces (including, of course, Spanish forces) were fighting a last ditch battle there with some hope of success, would raise the morale of underground resistance forces all over Europe. Thus Spain might play a role similar to that played by Great Britain during World War II—as an ultimate physical and psychological strongpoint from which the tide of battle could be turned.

Of the three armed services, the Spanish navy is currently the most valuable to NATO. Spain has a naval tradition, the navy is more "professional" than the army, and its thirty-five major combatants and 57,000 sailors and marines make it fourth in size among West European navies—just behind Italy's and just ahead of West Germany's.[2] Spain's geographic location at the narrow juncture of the Mediterranean and Atlantic adds utility to her naval strength, as does her possession of two strategic island groups in the approaches to the Straits—the Canary Islands in the Atlantic and the Balearic Islands in the Mediterranean. However, the Navy can hardly be considered a net increment to NATO's naval strength as a consequence of Spanish membership, since for some time it has been informally coordinated with other NATO naval forces in the area. Formal integration might create more political trouble than it was worth militarily, especially if it involved giving Spain a role in the IBERLANT (Iberian-Atlantic) command, now controlled by a jealous Portugal.

In time, Spain's army of 320,000, although it is scheduled to be reduced, could add significantly to NATO's conventional strength. Its basic role would be simply to defend its home territory. However, if properly trained and equipped, it could also be given a role in support of other countries on the southern front—Italy, Greece, and

Turkey—that are more vulnerable to invasion. There has been some discussion of Spanish participation in the new "ACE Mobile Force," designed as a small fast-acting task force to deal with specific emergencies on the northern or southern flanks of NATO.[3]

It is also conceivable that Spanish ground forces could assist on the central front. In this role they would function most usefully as reinforcement units, stationed in peacetime on their home territory and deployed in West Germany during wartime, or during a crisis, according to contingency plans. Spain's impressive pool of over one million trained reservists could make an additional contribution.[4]

An important domestic benefit from any of these roles would be the professionalizing and "taming" effects of giving the Spanish army an important external function in association with other NATO armies. The army's traditional orientation is toward internal security and domestic politics; the possibility of another *coup d'état* is a latent anxiety of the fledgling democracy. The assumption that merely giving the army an external role will divert it from domestic politics is perhaps too facile, but it is plausible in conjunction with a gradual socialization of the entire population to democratic values.

Any of the suggested roles for Spanish ground forces (and their professionalizing byproduct) would benefit the whole alliance to the extent that they increased the alliance's overall military capability: the benefits to Spain would be derivative from that. Most of them, however, would require the integration of Spanish forces within NATO's command structure, which the government has promised to avoid. On the other hand, as the French have demonstrated, a good deal of informal cooperation is possible outside the military command organization. It might be arranged through the higher-level political organs of the alliance—for example, the Defense Planning Committee. Or, if the U.S. base agreement is renewed in some form in 1988, it could occur bilaterally with the United States acting as agent for the alliance. Indeed, Spain's naval forces are already coordinated with NATO's naval commands via this latter route. However, the Socialist regime would be constrained in pursuing such stratagems by a suspicious left wing which has already accused the government of surreptitiously "cheating" on this condition of the referendum.[5]

The value to NATO of Spain's military forces is on the rise because of an increased interest among the West European members in building up the alliance's conventional strength. This interest is fundamentally the result of growing doubts about the credibility of the U.S. nuclear deterrent now that the Soviets have achieved parity, if not superiority, in intercontinental nuclear capability. These doubts have been strengthened by the recent "pre-summit" at Reykjavik where the United States appeared ready to accept such deep cuts in its strategic forces as to virtually eliminate their deterrent value for Europe. The Soviet-U.S. agreement to eliminate the recently deployed intermediate-range missiles, which many Europeans had been counting on to shore up the sagging U.S. deterrent and relieve them of the heavy costs of a conventional buildup has added new doubts. The apparently strong U.S. commitment to ballistic missile defenses (the Strategic Defense Initiative) implies a further weakening of nuclear deterrence. Europeans have also perceived a growing impatience in the U.S. Congress with European foot-dragging in meeting conventional force goals, which could activate new pressures for U.S. troop withdrawals.[6] For all these reasons, a strengthening of conventional forces in Europe has suddenly acquired a new urgency. Other European NATO members would welcome any contribution from Spain.

Spain's third condition for remaining in NATO was that the U.S. naval and air operations presently based in Spain be substantially reduced. This would have to be counted as a cost for the alliance, and derivatively for Spain, although not necessarily as a result of Spain's NATO membership per se, since the anti-American feeling that is behind the pressure for reduction would exist in any case. The cost would be the financial expense of moving the facilities, and presumably their reduced effectiveness in alternate locations— Portugal, Morocco, and Turkey have been mentioned. Spain's principal demands in the current negotiations are the removal of the seventy-two F-16 fighters and 5,000 U.S. servicemen now based at Torrejón, just outside Madrid, and a reduction in the 7,500 U.S. personnel now stationed at three other bases and various smaller facilities. The United States has offered to substitute Spaniards for Americans in support staff jobs and to move the F-16s to Seville, outside the range of Madrid's vociferous left-wing protesters. The negotiations are presently stalled, with the United States hinting at complete withdrawal and Spain threatening to let the base agreement lapse when it comes up for renewal in 1988.

Incidentally, France has recently weighed in on the U.S. side in this bargaining. President Mitterrand reminded Premier González, during a visit in March 1987, that the impending Euromissile deal between the Soviet Union and the United States would make the alliance more dependent on the conventional air-naval power that the United States wants to keep in Spain.[7]

Of course, the balance of costs and benefits must also include political values, since these were apparently decisive in prompting

Spain to join NATO, and later to stay in. Here the benefits are potentially great. Spain's overwhelming foreign policy goal is readmission to the community of democratic nations after being ostracized for forty years. Membership in both NATO and the European Community (EC) are both giant steps toward that goal. The payoffs are, first, the psychic value of being accepted, of ending her "national loneliness," and second, the consolidation of her new democratic institutions by linking them to a larger whole. In the case of NATO, what Spain really wanted was not membership in a military alliance, especially a U.S.-dominated one, but admission to the "Western alliance"—that great complex of culture, tradition, political institutions, etc., that centers in Western Europe and for which NATO serves as a symbolic core. NATO itself was probably negatively valued, but joining it was the price that had to be paid for full access to these broader values. The qualifications that were attached to Spanish membership were an attempt to drive the price as low as possible, or down to the maximum permitted by domestic constraints.

Spain as a Semialigned Country

The conditions with which Spain has hedged her membership in NATO make her one of the alliance's "semialigned" members. The posture of semialignment, as defined by Nils Orvik, refers to "states which are formally aligned, but which have made certain explicit reservations as to the degree of involvement in the alliance."[8] Such reservations, according to Orvik, may include refusals to accept nuclear weapons on national territory, the barring of foreign troops and bases, restrictions on NATO maneuvers and exercises on one's territory, and a low level of GNP allocated to defense.[9] I would add two more categories: refusal to participate in NATO's integrated military planning and command organization, and perception of the primary threat to the state's security from some source other than the Soviet Union. Note that all of these categories are limitations on a country's participation in NATO's primary mission: deterrence of and defense against Soviet military attack. They do not include a failure to follow the U.S. lead, or deviation from alliance policy generally, on political or economic issues, as during the Polish or pipeline crises of the early 1980s.

The Scandinavian members of NATO (Norway and Denmark) are semialigned by virtue of their rejection of nuclear weapons, bases, and foreign forces on their territories, a posture which they have held since the very beginning of the alliance—primarily out of fear of provoking the Soviets. Their military budgets are also low compared to those of most other members.[10] France is semialigned because of her formal nonparticipation in NATO's command structure and collective military planning, although she does cooperate informally in some ways.[11] Greece does not permit nuclear weapons on her soil, refuses to integrate her armed forces into NATO military commands, and participates in NATO exercises to only a limited degree. She does lease military and naval facilities to the United States for NATO purposes, but this U.S. presence is unpopular and U.S. use of the bases is subject to numerous restrictions.[12] Greece is semialigned also because she does not perceive NATO's opponent—the Soviet Union—as the primary threat to her own security, but rather, Turkey, another NATO member.

It is instructive to consider Spain's motives for semialignment compared to the other countries named. For example, the primary motive of Denmark and Norway in barring nuclear weapons and NATO bases and forces from their soil is to avoid provoking the Soviet Union, and this motive arises largely from their geographic proximity to the Soviets.[13] Spain, under no direct threat from the Soviets, bars these weapons for quite different reasons, more akin to those of the left-wing antinuclear movements in West Germany, Britain, and the Low Countries: nuclear weapons are inherently evil and their deployment on one's territory may lead to entrapment in a nuclear war that is generated out of a spiral of autonomous superpower hostility. Moreover, nuclear weapons are controlled by the United States and thus are an instrument for the perpetuation of U.S. domination of the alliance and its members. Antinuclearism is hardly distinguishable from anti-Americanism in Spain; that is not the case in the Nordic countries where it stems much more from pragmatic security concerns.

Spain's motives for nonparticipation in the NATO military organization are also different from those of France, Norway, and Denmark. Spain and France have in common the desire to assert their independence, but this desire stems from somewhat different emotional roots. In Spain it is primarily a left-wing phenomenon, strongly associated with anti-Americanism: NATO is perceived as a cover for U.S. imperialism and the organizational superstructure as an instrument of imperial control. In France, of course, it is a Gaullist phenomenon, but with nationwide support, and it is associated not so much with a virulent anti-Americanism as with nationalism and the drive for *grandeur*. And of course, France's nonparticipation is backstopped by her independent nuclear deterrent. The limited participation of the Nordic countries derives mainly from a cautiousness about being caught up in conflicts unrelated to their interests, a motive that is less prominent for Spain or France.

Spain's limitations on her alignment are similar to Greece's in many respects although the motivations are somewhat different. Her ban on nuclear weapons is motivated principally by pacifist sentiment and an apparent belief that she may thus avoid being a nuclear target; Greece rejects them mostly for the same reason that the Nordic countries do—to avoid provoking the Soviets—although left-wing antinuclearism in the ruling Socialist party no doubt reinforces geographical proximity as a motive. Spain refuses to formally integrate her forces into NATO's military commands primarily out of anti-American sentiment and her perception that NATO is a vehicle for U.S. domination; Greece refuses chiefly because of her conflicts with Turkey and her belief that the United States and NATO have not adequately supported her in these conflicts. She has limited her participation in NATO military exercises for the same reason.[14] Although Greece places severe restraints on U.S. use of her military and naval facilities, there does not seem to be the same degree of popular pressure to oust the United States completely, as exists in Spain. This difference is also explainable in geographical terms: Greece necessarily perceives a greater threat from the Soviet Union than Spain does, even though Turkey is seen as a more immediate threat; moreover, the aid that Greece receives in return for the bases is extremely valuable in prosecuting her conflicts with Turkey. The only one of the six criteria on which Greece clearly does not qualify as semialigned is defense expenditures: at 6.9 percent of GNP (1983), she is second only to the United States at 7.4 percent, compared to the Spanish figure of 2.4 percent.[15] This difference is attributable again to the Greek-Turkish conflict and to Spain's generally low degree of threat-perception.

The two countries have in common that they both perceive their principal security threat as emanating from a source other than the Soviet Union. In Spain's case, it is, curiously, Morocco. This threat arises from the vulnerability of two Spanish enclaves in Morocco: Ceuta, directly across the Straits from Gibraltar, and Melilla. Some 19,000 Spanish troops are detailed to guard each of these two towns and their environs against a Moroccan takeover.[16]

Spain and Greece also share the historical experience of having fairly recently emerged from a period of corrupt, authoritarian rule, although in Greece's case (the "Colonels' regime," 1967-1974) the period was much shorter. The perception of U.S. and NATO collaboration with those regimes is responsible for a good deal of the anti-American and anti-NATO feeling in both countries.

In all the countries mentioned, except France, there is a strong correlation between their semialigned stances and rule by socialist parties. Although nonsocialist parties in the Nordic states have supported semialignment, specific measures of noncooperation have all been initiated by socialist regimes. For both the socialists and the nonsocialists the central motive has been that of avoiding provocation of the Soviets. For the nonsocialists, geographical proximity to the Soviet Union is enough to dictate circumspection, consequently acquiescence in socialist-sponsored semialignment policies. The socialists, however, are motivated in addition by an ideologically rooted conviction that international conflict usually is caused by emotional "provocation" between states rather than by conflicting interests or inherent aggressiveness. The belief is widespread in Norway that the Soviets do not constitute an inherent threat: they are dangerous only if provoked.[17]

This emphasis on the causal importance of "provocation" and de-emphasis of deterrence (which requires a belief that the adversary is autonomously aggressive) is typical of the "idealist" approach to international conflict which (for reasons that are not well understood) is congenial to a socialist-party orientation. It is shared in the abstract by many Spanish socialists. But in Spain's case, this ideological predilection is not reinforced by the geographical nearness of a powerful opponent. Consequently the "avoid provocation" theme is weak in the Spanish worldview. Instead it is distance from, rather than proximity to, the major adversary that supports the semialigned stance of socialist Spain. Since the Soviet Union is so far away, it is not a serious threat: consequently the alliance is not worth much to Spain: consequently the risks of semialignment are small.

It is interesting to note the differences in the conditions placed on Spanish membership by the centrist party, the Unión del Centro Democrático (UCD), that took Spain into NATO in 1982 and the socialist party, the Partido Socialista Obrero Español (PSOE), which finally decided to keep her in. The UCD's conditions did not amount to semialignment; that party was willing to undertake full NATO participation provided only that some progress was being made on negotiations for Spanish entry into the EC and the transfer of Gibraltar to Spanish sovereignty.[18] The PSOE's conditions, however, do amount to a particularly stringent form of semialignment. They seem to be motivated chiefly by idealist/ideological sentiments such as those mentioned earlier, plus a large admixture of plain anti-Americanism.

The concept of "semialignment" is defined by Orvik in terms of the central military-security concerns and activities of the alliance. It could be expanded to include the degree of conformity to the alliance leader's desires on political and economic issues, including the "out-of-area" problems that so often place the United States at odds with its allies. By this broadened criterion, almost all the European allies are less than fully aligned. The United States has become accustomed to European nonconformity on Third World issues, notably in the Middle East, and on politico-economic relations with the Soviet Union. Spain is not likely to be an exception to this pattern. Even under the relatively cooperative Franco regime, Spain denied landing rights to U.S. planes engaged in resupplying Israel during the 1973 Yom Kippur war, cooperated only reluctantly in refueling U.S. F-15 planes during the Iranian crisis of 1979,[19] and refused permission for U.S. use of her airspace in the 1986 bombing strike against Libya. Given her high level of popular anti-Americanism and her relatively low security needs, Spain is indeed likely to be a leading NATO maverick. Her Arab and Latin-American "vocations," however insubstantial they may be, will no doubt strengthen tendencies toward independence from, and opposition to, U.S. policy outside Europe.

Semialignment is possible in NATO for reasons that arise ultimately from the bipolar structure of the international system. It is possible, first, because of the smorgasbord of degrees and kinds of participation from which members can select. This variegated menu is available because of the alliance's multilayered bureaucracy and because of the superpower leader's need to station forces in peacetime near the probable theatre of battle. Both the bureaucracy and the overseas stationing of U.S. forces are in turn a function of the permanence of rivalry between the superpowers, which is a structural phenomenon more than anything else. Semialignment is possible, secondly, because those states that shirk alliance "duties," or fail to heed the wishes of the alliance leader, need not fear serious reprisal, in particular the ultimate reprisal of withdrawal of protection. The reason is, again, structural: in a bipolar system, the superpowers will defend virtually any state within their strategic orbit against attack by the opposite superpower, whether they are formally allied with the state or not, and if allied, no matter how little the state contributes to the common enterprise.

To see these points more clearly, consider whether the intensity of peacetime collaboration that we observe in NATO would have been possible in the pre-1914 alliances. Though, of course, there were British-French and German-Austrian military staff talks and some cooperative planning from about 1905 onwards, it was very superficial collaboration compared to NATO's (and the Warsaw Pact's), and there was no stationing of forces on allied territory during peacetime. Partly this was a function of more primitive technology and a crude balance between adversaries that provided time for Allied forces to be deployed and coordinated after a war had begun. But it also followed from the distinct possibility that the ally of today might be the enemy of tomorrow. Since alliances were so easily reversible their members did not develop the expectation of permanency that today makes possible an alliance-wide superstructure of roles and missions from which members may choose their preferred range of activities. And of course there was no supertechnology like nuclear weapons, possessed by some and not by others, which not only protected but also threw the shadow of doom over those who harbored them. And finally, any shirking of obligations to allies was inhibited by the real possibility that it might alienate them and precipitate their defection.

Semialignment can be explained further in terms of the theory of "collective" or "public" goods.[20] In any alliance of states facing a common opponent (which may be another alliance) the security "produced" by the alliance is enjoyed by all members (and also by nonmembers threatened by the same opponent) no matter how much they each contribute to it; moreover, the security "consumed" by one does not appreciably diminish the security of others. Alliances in a bipolar system have the additional characteristic that the alliance leader will provide the public good in its own interest regardless of (within limits) how much the smaller members contribute toward it. Thus, the latter can refuse to perform what the alliance leader might consider their fair share of alliance tasks with no loss of benefits. Moreover, since the good that is provided by the leader is available to non-members as well as members, there is little or no cost in bringing in new members, even when it can be expected that they will contribute little to the common good. Thus, Spain is acceptable as a new member of NATO despite the limits she has placed on her participation.

Of course, the reality does not quite fit the theory, which merely states a logical tendency. In NATO, the lesser states do contribute something to the common enterprise—the semialigned states least, the other European members somewhat more, though none as much as the United States thinks they ought to contribute. They do so probably for three main reasons: (1) there is some indeterminate limit to the alliance leader's willingness to provide the collective good in its own interest; at some threshold point of non-contribution by others, it will prefer to withdraw rather than continue providing the good at increasing cost to itself; (2) it is humiliating for the smaller states to be too dependent on their superpower protector; and (3) every state will want to possess a certain amount and kind of military force simply as a badge of its sovereignty and to deal with situations not covered by the alliance contract.

The theory of collective goods would predict that the contributions of the alliance followers, in terms both of resources and risk-acceptance, is a function of their relative power. That is, the medium states in the alliance should logically contribute proportionately more than the weaker ones, including the four small semialigned states considered here. The reason is that when they shirk or renege they are more likely to push the superpower below its limits of tolerance because their expected contribution is larger—therefore they are less willing to take the risk. The evidence supports this logic. Great Britain, West Germany, and Italy are all more cooperative with the United States on the nonbudgetary measures of degree-of-alignment than the four small semialigned states. France, as usual, is a special case. As noted earlier, while she is semialigned in her non-participation in NATO commands and nonacceptance of U.S. nuclear weapons, bases, and forces, she is not "free riding" as much as the weaker semialigned states because she is a nuclear power in her own right, and her annual defense expenditures are among the highest in Europe. The generalization holds also for budgetary contributions: if we eliminate Greece, whose defense budget is bloated by her confrontation with Turkey, the weak states of NATO (including Spain) contributed, on the average, 2.28 percent of their GNP for defense in 1983, compared to an average of 3.9 percent for the four medium powers. The weak states spent $206 per capita on defense; the medium powers, $342.[21]

The theory of collective goods also says that shirkers gain more, the fewer other shirkers there are. This is because the total amount of the collective good—in NATO, the total amount of security—is higher the more parties contribute their "fair" share; the one or few states that then "defect" into semialignment enjoy more security than when many defect. Thus France's gain from nonparticipation in NATO commands is highest when all others—at least all the other midsize states—do participate, and would evaporate if they did not. Spain probably benefits, on balance, by refusing to accept U.S. nuclear submarines in her ports, and might benefit by expelling U.S. forces and bases—but only if others did accept them. Thus free riders like Spain are free riding not only on the U.S. but on their European partners as well.

The example of Spain demonstrates another point about

collective goods: they will be valued differently by different consumers. Spain, perceiving little or no threat from the Soviet Union, values the security good provided by NATO much lower than, say, The Federal Republic of Germany does. Therefore, Spain finds it easier to reduce her contribution. A state like the FRG could free ride in some way if it were confident the superpower protector would continue providing the ride, but its costs would be great if the confidence proved to be misplaced. Of course, Spain's low threat-perception may be largely a function of the presence of NATO forces, nuclear weapons, etc. on the territory of the FRG, in which case the point reduces to something like the previous one: the gain from free riding depends on others not doing it.

We may conclude that semialignment is an alliance posture that reflects three broad sets of causal factors: the structure of the bipolar security system; domestic politics; and particular factors, such as the relative power of the state, conflicts with other states, and geographical location, that mediate between the systemic and the domestic tendencies. The system makes a free (or cheap) ride possible, the domestic political pattern determines the degree of predilection for taking it, and the particular factors determine the actual price and value of the ride. These three sources of causation are probably central to the explanation of most kinds of international behavior; I have merely attempted here to spell out their relevance to the kind of behavior that Orvik and his collaborators have so usefully labeled "semialigned." For Spain, incidentally, the system is at least as permissive as for others in this category, and the domestic party in charge strongly favors a minimum of cooperation, so that Spain is potentially the "least aligned" of the states considered. Where she will actually stand on the spectrum of alignment in the near future will depend on how the U.S. base issue is resolved. Because of the relative absence of the particular geographical and conflictual constraints that affect the Nordic states and Greece, her alignment stance may be less stable than theirs since it will be more sensitive to shifts in the domestic power balance.

A European Defense "Entity"?

Some analysts worry about the disintegrative effects on NATO of taking on members such as Spain and Greece who seem to hinder more than they support the alliance's goals. Will not other members such as the Low Countries, observing such independence going unpunished, become more independent and obstructionist themselves, and could NATO survive such a "disintegrative spiral"? A question-begging answer is that it will survive so long as the United States tolerates such behavior. More to the point is that the United States will tolerate a great deal of it, since it has no real alternative, given its own interests that follow from the bipolar distribution of world power. Much of the anxiety about the possible breakup of NATO stems from a failure to recognize the difference between NATO (and the Warsaw Pact) and alliances in the multipolar systems of the past. The latter could and sometimes did collapse under too much policy divergence among their members; they were created in the first place out of temporary similarities of interest and policy rather than structural necessities and when these similarities evaporated, the alliances lost their value and their members abandoned each other for other partners. Since a bipolar alliance such as NATO is built on a structural foundation rather than a temporary convergence of policies, it can survive such policy diversity among its members. Theoretically, it will survive until the bipolar structure of power is transformed into some other structure. However, this is a theoretical conclusion that Europeans should beware of taking too literally. As a nuclear great power separated from Europe by 3,000 miles of water, the United States is not as powerfully subject to structural determinism as it would be if it were territorially contiguous to Europe in a non-nuclear world. In other words, the U.S. commitment to Western Europe does not depend so much on danger to its own physical security if the Soviets were to conquer Western Europe, as on other values that are less compelling and more changeable than security. Thus, it is conceivable that at some point in a progressive European shirking of what the United States considers its alliance "duties," the U.S. anger at being exploited might overcome its stake in preserving democratic-capitalist institutions in Western Europe, and provoke it to withdraw both its troops and its nuclear umbrella.

Europeans have had some reason lately to worry about such U.S. abandonment. The portents include the obvious "unilateralism" of the Reagan administration; its apparent indifference to Europe compared to Third World issues; strong support in the Senate for the Nunn amendment of 1984, which proposed a one-third reduction in U.S. troop levels in Europe unless the European allies met agreed NATO defense-spending increases; and the isolationist overtones of the Strategic Defense Initiative. The Soviet achievement of nuclear parity has raised the possibility of "nuclear abandonment," not by a deliberate U.S. withdrawal of its nuclear commitment, but rather by the undermining of its effectiveness. The latter worry was given a tremendous fillip by the 1986 arms control proceedings at Reykjavik, where the U.S. president appeared willing to give up virtually all of the U.S. capability for extended deterrence in Europe.

One result of these developments has been an increased European interest in some kind of autonomous West European defense entity.[22] Items in this trend include the reactivation of the Western European Union (WEU) under French leadership, increased activity by the European Political Community (EPC), the vehicle for foreign policy collaboration among members of the EC, and steadily increasing military collaboration between France and Germany, and more recently, between France and Great Britain. The latter two countries have been drawn closer together by the logic of a possible superpower agreement to eliminate intermediate-range missiles and to reduce long-range strategic missiles by 50 percent or more. The logic points toward increased cooperation between (if not "integration" of) the French and British nuclear forces as a substitute for the weakened U.S. deterrent. The Europeans are also increasing their cooperation at more mundane levels, such as the joint production of military equipment.

All this does not mean that a united Western Europe is around the corner, but at least the notion of a "European pillar" within NATO is being revived in tangible form. Its relevance for our present theme is that Spain has indicated clearly that she would rather associate with a European defense entity than with NATO. Presumably, as a member of NATO, she will be more willing to collaborate militarily with a European grouping within NATO than with the NATO military commands. She would then avoid the "U.S. domination" that many Spaniards associate with the NATO command structure; at the same time she could realize, and the whole alliance would realize, many of the military and political benefits discussed earlier that depend on military cooperation with her neighbors. As a member of the EC, but not WEU, Spain may prefer the EPC as the vehicle for West European politico-military collaboration. However, other European members of NATO would rather cooperate through WEU on military issues, and Spain has shown some interest in joining that organization.[23]

An interesting possibility is that Spain and France might decide to coordinate their forces more formally and closely than either coordinates with NATO. Both would retain their precious independence from U.S. influence while benefiting militarily from collaboration, and psychologically from an easing of their sense of isolation. France would gain advantages of strategic depth and a promise of early Spanish reinforcement if Soviet troops crossed the Franco-

German boundary. Spain would benefit from the professionalizing of her officer corps that would result from close association with their French counterparts. If linked up with the slowly developing Franco-German military collaboration, it might be an important step toward realization of the Gaullist dream of leadership of a loosely confederated Europe. Similarities of language and culture, and of geography (France and Spain are the only two European countries that have both Atlantic and Mediterranean coastlines) add some plausibility to the notion. French-Spanish military cooperation has developed considerably since Spain's democratization: the two countries have held joint naval maneuvres and joint army exercises in the Pyrenees, they have initiated plans for joint defense production, and they have cooperated in combating Basque terrorism.

Conclusion

Given the constraints that Spain has imposed on her alliance participation, the military-security payoff from her membership in NATO—to herself and to other members—is at best problematical. There are a number of potentially significant benefits, but realizing them will require a higher degree of collaboration between Spanish forces and the NATO military organization than currently seems likely. Informal cooperation will no doubt occur, but it will be narrowly constrained by domestic politics—in particular the sensitivities and suspicions of the ruling Socialist party's rank-and-file. There may even be a net cost to the alliance if the current negotiations continue about U.S. base rights result in their termination or sharp reduction.

However, the political gains over the long run will probably be substantial. Having been ostracized from democratic Europe for four decades, and having now corrected the reason for it, Spain desperately wants to be reaccepted as a full member of the Western democratic community. The other European states, and the United States as well, have every reason to welcome her, for they have their own interests (which are not without their security implications) in nurturing Spanish democracy. Spain's formal association with NATO and the EC obviously promotes this shared interest. In time, once she has regained her national self-confidence and a sense of acceptance, her objections to military integration may decline.

For the present, the limits on Spain's participation in NATO activities place her in the category of "semialigned" states within the alliance. She differs somewhat from others in that class in that her posture is so clearly the result of a straddle between domestic political constraints and external *political* goals, rather than military-security ones. Alliance membership and participation is more important as it mediates between external and internal political needs than for what it entails in security benefits, risks, and costs. And because much of the payoff from the external goals is ultimately domestic (for example, the "taming of the military"), the alliance functions largely as an instrument or strategy in domestic politics. For the political center in Spain—including the leadership of the PSOE—alliance membership is above all valued as a means of stabilizing the new democratic institutions. This means principally weakening the vestiges of a reactionary past, but paradoxically, the government is hindered in the pursuit of this goal by the prejudices and power of a radical Left which opposes the degree of NATO participation that would significantly advance the goal. The government cannot risk alienating the Left, for that might push the radicals into the streets, where they would pose their own threat to democracy, perhaps by precipitating a Right-Left polarization. Thus Spain's semialignment is at bottom a domestic political compromise which optimizes the prospects for domestic stabilization. Spain's alliance partners would be wise, for the moment, not to try to push her into a closer association, for the survival of Spanish democracy is in their interest as well.

Because of strong anti-American and anti-NATO sentiment in Spain, she is likely to be a supporter of the recent movement toward an autonomous European defense grouping. It will be psychologically and politically easier for her to cooperate militarily with such a group than with NATO commands. The prospect of firmly linking Spanish forces, especially ground forces, to the defense of Western Europe through such an organization may stimulate the larger countries to push ahead with the project. There is no good reason for the United States to resist this trend, especially since it seems to be oriented toward increasing conventional forces. If European free riding is the problem, they may be less likely to do it if it is clear they are riding on each other.

Notes

1. Max G. Manwaring and Alan Ned Sabrosky, "Iberia's Role in NATO's Future: Strategic Reserve, Reinforcement, and Redoubt." *Parameters*, 16, no. 1 (Spring, 1986), pp. 43-55. See also Hal Klepak, *Spain: NATO or Neutrality?*, National Security Series 1/80 (Kingston, Ontario: Queens University, 1980).

pp. 1-50, for an early discussion of the security implications of Spanish membership.
2. International Institute of Strategic Studies, London, *The Military Balance, 1985-1986*, p. 58.
3. Gregory Treverton, "Spain: Domestic Politics and Security Policy," International Institute of Strategic Studies, *Adelphi Papers*. no. 204 (1986), p. 37. This monograph is the best recent discussion of Spain's role in NATO and related issues.
4. International Institute of Strategic Studies, p. 57.
5. *The Manchester Guardian*. September 27, 1986, 6:3.
6. International Institute of Strategic Studies, *Strategic Survey, 1985-1986*, pp. 36-37.
7. *The Economist*, March 21, 1987, p. 62.
8. Nils Orvik, ed., *Semialignment and Western Security* (New York: St. Martin's Press, 1986), p. 6. Orvik and his collaborators do not include Spain among NATO's semialigned countries, perhaps owing to uncertainty about Spain's membership when the book was written.
9. Ibid., p. 10.
10. Carsten Holbraad, "Denmark: Half-Hearted Partner," and Nils Orvik, "Norway: Deterrence Versus Nonprovocation," in Ibid., pp. 61-108 and 186-248.
11. Orvik does not include France in his list of semialigned countries because of her greater power, her independent nuclear forces and her military activity outside Europe. In my view, these qualities do distinguish France from the smaller countries, but not on the basic criteria for "semialignment." See Orvik, *Semialignment and Western Security*, p. 11.
12. Constantine Melakopides, "Greece: From Compliance to Self-Assertion," in Orvik, *Semialignment and Western Security*, pp. 81-108. For the restrictions on U.S. use of the bases, see p. 84.
13. Carsten Holbraad, Ruud Koale, Paul Lucardie, Constantine Melakopides, Christopher Rose, and Hugh Thorburn, "The Reality of Semialignment," in Orvik, *Semialignment and Western Security*, p. 268.
14. Melakopides, pp. 73-74.
15. International Institute of Strategic Studies, *The Military Balance*, p. 170.
16. Treverton, p. 22.
17. These statements are based on Orvik's and Holbraad's analysis of Norway and Denmark, but go somewhat beyond their interpretations in distinguishing between the socialists' and nonsocialists' motivations. See Orvik, *Semialignment and Western Security*, pp. 15-61 and 186-248.
18. Paul Preston and Denis Smyth, *Spain, The EEC and NATO*, The Royal Institute of International Affairs, Chatham House Papers no. 22 (London: Routledge & Kegan Paul, 1984), p. 70.
19. Treverton, p. 17.
20. Gregory Treverton has applied this theory to NATO in a nontechnical way in *Making the Alliance Work: The United States and Western Europe* (Ithaca: The Cornell University Press, 1985). pp. 12-25. The classic treatise on the subject is Mancur Olson, *The Logic of Collective Action* (Cambridge: Harvard University Press, 1965). The first application of the theory to NATO was Mancur Olson, Jr. and Richard Zeckhauser, "An Economic Theory of Alliances," *The Review of Economics and Statistics* 48, no. 3 (August 1966). pp. 266-279.

21. The average for the medium states would be considerably higher if it were not for the low defense expenditures of Italy: 2.8 percent of GNP and $172 per capita. Data are from International Institute of Strategic Studies, *The Military Balance*, p. 170.

22. James M. Markham, "U.S.-Soviet Missile Talks Pull Europeans Together," *New York Times*, March 22, 1987, p. E3; Peter H. Langer, *Transatlantic Discord and NATO's Crisis of Decision* (Washington: Pergamon-Brassey's, 1986). p. 86; Geoffrey Lee Williams and Alan Lee Williams, *The European Defense Initiative* (New York: St. Martin's Press, 1986).

23. The possibility of a Paris-Madrid axis is discussed in Klepak, p. 111.

10

Epilogue

Joseph S. Tulchin

The definition of Spain's position within the western alliance has been hostage for several years to the bilateral talks with the United States over U.S. bases on Spanish soil. Despite protestations by the Spanish government that the two issues were separate, both the United States and the principal NATO allies saw them as one. On the domestic front, prominent members of the opposition as well as the broader public have had trouble distinguishing between the two issues. The precise nature of Spain's relations with the alliance were virtually on hold until the fate of the U.S. bases in Spain had been determined. If anything, there had been a slight hardening of the positions taken by France, Germany, and Great Britain with reference to Spanish participation in the joint military command, Spanish obligations to the alliance, and Spanish access to decisionmaking within the alliance. There is even evidence that these difficulties have spilled over into talks on issues under discussion within the European Community (EC). Like it or not, the Spanish government found the bilateral talks with the United States over the bases on Spanish territory blocking the way to progress in the slow process of Spain's reinsertion into the Western community of nations. The outcome of the talks on the bases undoubtedly will shape the role that Spain plays within NATO and on the world stage, including the evolution of its so-called special relationship with Latin America.

The recently concluded treaty between the Soviet Union and the United States limiting intermediate-range nuclear weapons, threatens to harden even further the European stance with reference to Spanish obligations. Reduction in nuclear weapons in Europe and the reduction in European reliance upon nuclear weapons for their defense automatically increases the reliance upon conventional forces. The recent attention paid to the shift of Soviet submarines from the western Atlantic to the European theater only adds immediacy to the discussion. This has the effect of reducing the relative importance of U.S. strategic weapons and increasing the significance of European weapons and bases. The likelihood that tactical air groups will be shifted from Spain to some other point in Europe or simply eliminated—although this second option is extremely unlikely—is no longer a matter of concern only to the two parties directly involved in the negotiations, if it ever was. Under such pressure, older members of the alliance will be less tolerant of newer members who seek reduced or conditional military commitments. As one Belgian diplomat put it: "There can be only one Gaullist option, and it already has been done." Moreover, the new superpower treaty comes at a time when NATO is going through a testing transition from a long period of U.S. dominance to a new stage of shared influence. In such a stage, Spain's role can be especially important. Spain's leaders are mindful of the opportunity and talk boldly of making a significant contribution to the alliance based upon their fresh approach to East-West issues.

The U.S. government hoped that getting the NATO allies involved and increasing the pressure on Spain would soften the Spanish position. Instead, the Spanish appeared to toughen their stance, at least in rhetoric. In October 1987, for the first time, the Spanish government demanded a timetable for renegotiating the agreement or, failing such agreement, for withdrawal of U.S. air forces from Spanish territory. In December, as a reaction to what they perceived as foot-dragging by the U.S. negotiators, the Spanish declared that the bases would have to be removed by 1991, if agreement on renegotiation were not reached before that date. This caught the attention of the U.S. media. The year 1991 would have been appropriate for such action, as the Spanish government certainly did not want to allow the talks or even the withdrawal to drag on into 1992 when the entire world will be celebrating the 500th anniversary of Columbus' voyage to the New World, and when most of Spain will be engaged in some way with the celebrations planned for that year on the peninsula. That is the year, also, set as the target by the government for completing Spain's entry into the EC. The United States has not discarded its NATO card. As part of the January deal, Spain accepted the U. S. demand for a new, comprehensive, long-term defense treaty. Perhaps as the first salvo in the new round of talks, Secretary of State George Schultz told reporters that his government probably would have to sacrifice the F-16s of the 401st Tactical Air Wing, the largest U. S. unit in the Mediterranean, and that such a move would leave a hole in the southern defense of NATO.

Spain's membership in NATO has been a challenge to Felipe González, the president of the Spanish government and the head of the Spanish Socialist party, ever since he took power in 1982. The challenge has been twofold: domestic and international. On the domestic front, the Partido Socialista Obrero Español (PSOE) government has been trying to build support in the Center and on the Right, while maintaining its support on the Left of the Spanish political spectrum. This has been particularly difficult in the case of NATO, given that the Left, historically, has been suspicious of the Western democracies because of their failure to support the Republic during the Spanish Civil War, and has had no fear of the Soviet Union, stemming from the same historical experience in the Civil War. Certainly, this was the basis of the PSOE position when it was in the opposition. The party skillfully played on these historical memories in creating negative attitudes toward NATO among broad segments of the public. Once in power, the PSOE was hoist on its own pétard as it found itself hard pressed to alter the negative attitudes it had done so much to foster. Tension between the historical faction and the pragmatic faction within the party led to the first crisis in the new government. Fernando Morán was forced out as foreign minister in 1985, signaling the triumph of the pragmatists.

But, the historical faction continues to exercise considerable influence within the party and, judging from public opinion polls conducted by the government's Centro de Investigaciones Sociológicas (CIS), accurately represents strongly held views among the populace. As one member of the party's foreign policy staff told me: "None of the countries against which NATO's bases were pointed had ever been an enemy of Spain." Going further, he declared that "Spain was neither an Eastern nor a Western nation." In the next breath, he went on to indicate that "the United States, more than any other external force, contributed to the longevity of the Franco dictatorship," thus indicating how historical memory contributes to the ambivalence towards NATO and converges foreign policy issues. The bases are a legacy of the Franco era. Getting rid of them has been seen by many as a positive, even necessary, step in the consolidation of Spanish democracy.

But if the Left is ambivalent toward NATO, the Center and Center-Right have been immobilized by the PSOE switch. They were supporters of Spanish participation in NATO when the PSOE was in opposition. They remain cynical about the PSOE's shift in 1985 and the government's efforts to build a coalition of support for the idiosyncratic Spanish relationship to NATO. These internationalists, like the Partido Democrático Popular (PDP), and the factions of the Unión del Centro Democrático (UCD) and the Alianza Popular (AP) that favor an orthodox posture toward NATO, supported the entry into NATO from the very beginning. They cannot switch now. They struggled to criticize the government for the manner in which it has conducted negotiations. But they have a difficult political job. They desperately need foreign policy issues on which they can distinguish themselves publicly from the PSOE. However, they must be extremely careful that in ridiculing the government for failing to assume its responsibilities in NATO, they do not stir the powerful nationalist urges among their own partisans on the Right nor allow the government to declare itself the only true representative of Spanish nationalism. As Abril Martorell suggests, many of these people would be happy to have NATO act as a European mechanism to blunt the rivalry between the superpowers. Some critical figures within the government think the same way.[1]

Another domestic factor further complicating the assimilation into NATO is Spain's relative economic backwardness. Although much has been made of the Spanish economic miracle, Spain remains far behind the rest of Europe in many ways. In addition, José Maravall puts great emphasis on the relative rigidity of Spanish social structure. This combined with lower taxes and much lower social welfare benefits, only one half the EC average, make it difficult for Spain to meet EC standards. This is true also in matters of bringing backward Spanish infrastructure up to modern standards which are making talks between the EC and Spain more difficult as the years go on.[2]

Spanish membership in NATO is a challenge to the PSOE government on the international front because it is proving difficult to define a policy that is autonomous without being seen as odd or destructive. Linkage with the talks on the U.S. bases only has compounded these difficulties. By the same token, Spanish ambiguity on NATO made U.S. negotiators in the bases talks unsympathetic to Spanish requests for U.S. flexibility. The Spanish would have liked to deal with NATO and the bases as if they were separate issues, for various reasons, apart from the domestic political considerations already mentioned. First, it would have made the talks with the United States much easier and helped to justify the position taken with reference to the U.S. bases. Second, it would free the discussions with the NATO command of the heavy tone of Spanish nationalism that permeated the discussions with the United States regarding the bases. Spanish nationalism has been a powerful weapon in the talks with the United States, but it is a weapon that cannot always be controlled by the government. The rhythm of the talks with the United States was virtually dictated by the profound and varied sentiments of nationalism that stir deep anti-U.S. emotions on the political Right and on the Left. It is hard enough for the Felipe González government to conduct negotiations with the United States without being overcome by the nationalist mood. It would be impossible for the government to negotiate seriously with NATO under such pressure.

In general terms, the force of Spanish nationalism favors neutralism. It is a xenophobic force very near the surface in Spanish politics because of the long period of isolation from the rest of the world and the deep-seated sense of inferiority that is a legacy of that isolation. If such a force were to drive Spanish policy uncontrolled, it would undermine Spain's reentry into the Western world following nearly half a century of isolation. That, Felipe González is unwilling to let happen. Spain has committed itself to the West; it has no other viable option. It is the only way in which Spain can become a modern, democratic nation.

Ever since the end of the Civil War, Spain has held itself aloof or been held aloof from participation in the affairs of the European and north Atlantic nations. Reinsertion into the Western community as a democratic nation is the most comprehensive rejection of the Franco legacy in international affairs. Unable to participate in Western affairs, Franco constructed an elaborate foreign policy that was designed to make the best of Spain's isolation. It was a defensive posture, designed to trivialize international affairs precisely because Spain was unable to play a significant role in them. It accentuated the positive, the elements of Spain's glorious past, and its geographical position in the Mediterranean. According to this policy, Spain had a special relationship with Latin America and a vocation as a Mediterranean power, with advantages over the nations of Europe in relations with the Arab nations of North Africa and the Middle East. These were essentially symbolic positions for the Franco regime, devices to protect it from hostile surroundings.

With Franco's death, the defensive foreign policy that emphasized Spain's differences from the rest of Europe became a painfully negative element in the Franco legacy. As prime minister, Adolfo Suárez tried to turn the special relationship with Latin America and the Arab world into a positive factor by making them the unique feature of Spain's reinsertion into the Western community. Spain could bring that characteristic into the community. In Latin America particularly, Suárez was much taken by the reception he was given as he traveled through the region and honestly came to believe that Spain had a vocation as a spokesman for the Third World. But Spain did not have the resources to help the Third World and certainly was not going to become part of the Third World, so that option never could be used to define Spain's role among the world's nations.[3]

Successive governments have attempted to use Spain's role or potential role in Latin America as a device to expand Spain's presence in the international system. But that presence is circumscribed by a lack of resources, by skepticism on the part of certain groups in Latin America, and by the presence of U.S. power. The PSOE is sympathetic to efforts on the part of many Latin American governments to free themselves from U.S. hegemony and from East-West conflict. The Socialists feel they have a special relationship with the Sandinistas and the Fidelistas, focus of greatest tension, so that they can exercise leadership in the multilateral efforts to achieve peace in the region. Here, the limits to Spanish effectiveness are the lack of resources already mentioned, together with U.S. intransigence. Also, assertion of Spanish influence in the region inevitably puts Spain in conflict with the United States precisely at a time when the Spanish government would like to reduce tension with the U.S. government on all foreign policy issues so that the talks on the bases could proceed with few distractions. In the Middle East, it is improbable that Spain will play a significant role because the great powers are actively involved and leave no scope for Spanish initiatives. The PSOE feels it can exert some influence through the socialist parties in the region, but those parties appear to enjoy very little influence today.

In the final analysis, Spain must deal with its return to the world as a European nation, and as a European nation with much less effective power than most of its neighbors and allies. While this may not be an ideal situation or one that is flattering to Spanish pride, it is the most realistic. As a senior official in the Ministry of Foreign Affairs declared in an interview: "The transition stage in Spanish foreign policy is over. Spain is part of the West. It is defined as Western and is committed to Western values." This same official placed the greatest importance on the referendum in 1985 which confirmed the nation's commitment to the West. He recognized that Spanish reality includes the contradiction between wholehearted commitment to Europe and the fear of both superpowers. Working out the consequences of the referendum will serve to dissipate the contradiction over time. Joining NATO is not so much admitting that

Spain is part of a military alliance as it is part of the broader decision to join the West.

In order to maintain its new position in the West, the Spanish government must establish a viable, stable relationship with the NATO alliance. In order to do that, it must resolve its difficulties with the United States. It will not be easy and it will not happen quickly. As former prime minister Calvo Sotelo indicated, because of Spain's isolation from the West, the nation lacked a foreign policy tradition and is literally immature in its handling of foreign affairs.[4] One observer indicated that Spain had been marginal to world affairs not for fifty years, but for two hundred! It had been out of touch for so long that it would have to relearn how to participate in world affairs, to regain a sense of what the current issues were, who the players were, and what the rules of the game were. There is extensive evidence that, as the PSOE government accumulates experience in world affairs, it moves gradually toward pragmatic or moderate positions on major issues.[5]

Part of the process of reinsertion into the international community is a quickening of debate in Spain on foreign policy questions. Since Franco's death, several journals have appeared whose principal concern is foreign affairs. All of the major political parties have foreign policy spokesmen. The public press is concerned with the nation's international position, and the public opinion polls conducted monthly by CIS on behalf of the government now regularly include questions concerning foreign policy issues. Spain and Spain's role in the Western alliance have become topics of interest to centers of strategic studies in the United States and Great Britain. This debate has made plain that there are fundamental differences between Spanish perceptions of major issues and the perceptions of non-Spanish students of the same issues. Even when the issues are defined in strategic terms, which had not been the case in Spanish political discourse until very recently, those differences in perception hold.

One of the reasons put forward to explain Spain's reluctance to accept a full measure of military responsibility within NATO stems from its perception of a threat from the South. Former foreign minister Pérez Llorca told me that there were two "hot potatoes" issues which occupied his time in office: Spain's entry into Europe, and Morocco. He felt that in his negotiations with the officials of NATO there was too little appreciation of the fact that Spain was a nation of islands and that the NATO command made too few concessions to Spain's need to defend its outlying possessions.[6] Angel Viñas, perhaps the most prolific spokesman for the PSOE foreign policy, made a similar argument in claiming that NATO did not deal adequately with the most likely threats to Spanish security, which were from the south. In fact, according to Viñas, from the Spanish perspective the U.S. bases agreement does not deal adequately with any of these threats. As the chapters by Treverton and Snyder demonstrated, U.S. students of strategic issues have problems appreciating the Spanish perspective.

The problem, according to Viñas, is to reconcile existing NATO priorities with Spanish priorities. He asserts that Spain's security risks actually go up as it becomes a member of NATO. Such an assertion, based upon the attribution of equal risk to a variety of perceived threats, merely demonstrates the fragility of geopolitical calculations made without taking into account relative risk probability or the costs and benefits accruing to political decisions made in conjunction with military commitments. While it may be argued that in strictly military terms, and only in the short run, that Spain would run lower risks outside NATO than within the alliance, the political and, ultimately, the economic costs of remaining outside the alliance—pushing Spain back into a position of isolation from the rest of the West—would be unacceptably high. Privately, members of the PSOE government recognize this. Still, they persisted in making the same arguments in their diplomatic exchanges with the U.S. negotiators, driving more than one to declare, anonymously, to the press, that the Spanish did not understand the realities of modern international politics. Privately, one of the members of the U.S. team confided that he was convinced that the Spanish did not appreciate power realities in the world, that their isolation had distorted their perception of international relations. From my conversations with members of the Spanish team, I can state with confidence that this is not true. But, it remains clear that there have been serious problems of communication between the two teams of diplomats.

Once the decision was made to rejoin the Western world, the decision to enter NATO was almost inevitable. That is the great success of the Calvo Sotelo government in tying the hands of the incoming Socialists, in 1982. Calvo Sotelo and his foreign minister, José Pedro Pérez Llorca, succeeded in putting the critical decision about reentering Europe into dichotomous terms: in or out. Framed in such a manner, the decision was foreclosed. The PSOE could complain and criticize NATO, but when the time came they had to change their position and support entry into the alliance. As Inocencio Arias points out, it was not an easy decision and the referendum was very close. Having lost considerable face in changing its position on NATO, the Socialists attempted to recoup some of their political capital by assuming a strident tone in their early talks with the United States. The problem with that strategy was that the strident tone stimulated the deep-seated feelings of nationalism and anti-Americanism among a broad spectrum of the Spanish people. That, together with an unsympathetic posture by the senior U.S. negotiators, brought the talks to the brink of failure.

The Spanish relationship to NATO is also a challenge to the Spanish government in the formulation of its policies appropriate to the reinsertion of Spain in the Western world. Spain has not exercised a significant role in world affairs for many years. It has not participated at all in the Western power system during the twentieth century. Here, Abril Martorell and Tusell are correct in pointing us to Spanish history to understand the nation's foreign policy attitudes and to explain its foreign policies.

If Calvo Sotelo and Pérez Llorca succeeded in committing Spain to the West and to Europe by framing the discussion in dichotomous terms, in so doing, they contributed to the real difficulties confronting the current regime in attempting to formulate specific policies relevant to Spain's new position in the Western alliance. Spanish public opinion does not understand foreign policy questions in dichotomous terms. There are serious divisions among the Spanish public and within the various political parties on foreign policy issues.

Various studies of Spanish public opinion in the past decade have revealed a high degree of political alienation among the Spanish. José Maravall considers this a great danger to Spanish democracy because the political institutions are still so fragile. He fears that this alienation might drive Spain back to its isolation, and that confrontations over foreign policy issues, when those issues have been defined in dichotomous terms, increase the dangers.[8] Rupérez feels that the lack of experience in international affairs makes it difficult for the Spanish public to perceive national interests. He praised the UCD and Suárez for political skill and courage in getting the NATO treaty through the parliament in 1981, but he faulted Suárez for failing to make the issue clear to the public. That made it easy for the opposition, particularly PSOE, to criticize the move and to mount a strong, negative campaign against NATO. Now the PSOE government must deal with these negative feelings. For Rupérez, the solution is a matter of combining ill-founded, but definite, perceptions with a determined understanding of the nation's interests.[9] That, more or less, is the same position taken by professionals in the ministry and by members of Felipe's foreign policy team in Moncloa Palace, in discussing how to deal with Spanish public opinion.

The key to the collapse of the UCD in 1981/1982 is the failure to create a modern conservative party. López Pintor, relying on the same CIS polls as well as some of his own, says that in strictly ideological terms, the majority of the Spanish people are centrist or center-right, not leftist. He argues that direct contrast between Spanish political parties and parties in other European countries is difficult because most parties in Europe evolved out of the postwar reaction to the war and define their differences in terms of the war and the cold war. That certainly is not true of Spanish parties and, therefore, Spanish public opinion does not divide along lines similar to those that define political groups elsewhere in Europe, at least not on foreign policy issues.[10]

The most prickly foreign policy issue that divides Spanish public opinion differently from its European counterparts is the attitude toward the United States. As I have indicated at several points in this essay, there is deepseated hostility toward the United States on the Left and on the Right, and it even crops up in the Center. Recent public opinion studies demonstrate clearly that the overwhelming majority of the Spanish public takes the United States as its model or ideal lifestyle, and the portion of the Spanish public anxious to copy American ways of life is growing.[11] Positive feelings toward the United States or toward things American vary directly with education, income, and, except on the Left, with age. On the Left, the young aspire more than their elders to imitate the American way of life. Optimists might argue that these data represent evidence that over time the legacy of anti-Americanism inherited from the Franco regime will dissipate. On the other hand, the same polls show that the Spanish public persists in its even division between those who see the Soviet Union as the principal threat to world peace and those who see the United States as the principal threat. And that in a country that recently voted to join a military alliance directed against the Soviet Union!

There is a persistent knee-jerk anti-Americanism across the Spanish political spectrum that the government was not shy in using in its negotiations with the United States over the bases. It is a dangerous weapon, one that can turn into a boomerang and harm the government. The tactics used by the government in the final months of 1987 will make it much more difficult to convince the public to accept any settlement. Although members of the Spanish government deny vehemently that their actions were responsible for making it so, it seems clear that the bases became the critical issue in public debate on Spain's position in world affairs. They focused all of Spanish foreign policy attention and affected Spain's other policies or positions, as in Latin America, in the East-West confrontation.

The bilateral talks went badly. Private interviews with participants indicated that from the beginning the Spanish would accept the basic U. S. position. They would be content if the United States were to move its planes out of Torrejón, which is within walking distance for protest marchers from Madrid. This was a position the United States indicated it would accept. The Spanish declared publicly and privately that they did not seek the ouster of all U.S. forces from Spanish territory. Despite these protestations, U.S. observers, somehow continued to believe that this was the Spanish position. How could this have happened? It appears to have been the result of the nationalist rhetoric of the Spanish government and the personalities of the senior negotiators on the U.S. side. For many months, Secretary of Defense Caspar Weinberger refused to discuss the Spanish proposal, put forward informally, to close only the base at Torrejón and shift the aircraft stationed there to other bases on Spanish soil. Weinberger claimed that the move would be too costly and that he would not sanction such an expense while the administration was under pressure to cut the defense budget. One senior member of the U.S. team commented that Weinberger was less of a problem than Secretary of State Schultz, who complained to his staff that he was outraged by what he called the Spanish game of chicken. He would not be intimidated. He would show the Spanish what it was like to play hardball. This suggests that the bases talks became a classic case of negotiations that had every objective reason to succeed nearly failing because of imperfect communication among the negotiators and because of the personalities of the parties involved.

The NATO and bases issues are tied together in a complex manner that is embarrassing to the PSOE government. If the government shies away from NATO, it will have to tighten its ties to the United States. On the other hand, if it tries to loosen the U.S. ties, it must strengthen its ties to NATO, but that will have been made more difficult by the reduction of U.S. forces in Spain. Glenn Snyder suggests that Spain's alignment status is likely to continue to be a function of domestic political issues because of the absence of external constraints, the greater distance from the threat, and the fact that it is the latest entry into the alliance. That will be true only if we consider the bases issue to be a domestic political issue, which it is, and not an external constraint as well. I cannot go along with that. The bases issue goes to the heart of both Spanish domestic politics and Spain's definition of its reinsertion into the international community. The danger for the Spanish government in its dealings with the United States continues to be the youth and fragility of Spanish democracy. The PSOE must be careful not to undermine Spanish democracy in attempting to assert a new, powerful personality for Spain in international affairs. While the danger of totalitarian subversion may have diminished in the past few years, there remains the real danger that Spain will slip back into a grouchy isolation from the mainstream of Western affairs and be reduced to a semi-anarchy in domestic affairs and become crushingly inconsequential in international affairs.[12]

My own view is more optimistic. I have great confidence in the perception and pragmatism of Felipe González and his foreign policy team. I have confidence, too, in the growing resilience of Spanish democracy. I expect democratic Spain to play a major role in the Western alliance in the years to come. However, in order for that role to be effective, the Spanish must adjust some of their positions to the established mores of the alliance and become reconciled to a position slightly removed from the first rank of the allies. That may bruise national pride for a while, but compared to Spain's position in world affairs for the last half century or more, it is a giant step forward. Perhaps most optimistic of all, I anticipate that, with the bases negotiations virtually concluded, as Spain's position in NATO becomes regularized, hostility toward the United States will become less salient in domestic affairs, and another ghost of the Franco era will be laid to rest.

Notes

1. Juan Antonio Yáñez, "Relaciones entre Europa y Iberoamerica en el Marco de las Relaciones Norte-Sur y Este-Oeste," in Yáñez, et al., *Encuentro en la Democracia: Europa-Iberoamerica* (Madrid: ICI, 1986).

2. José Maravall, *The Transition to Democracy in Spain* (London: St. Martin's Press, 1982). On the economic miracle, see Eric N. Baklanoff, *The Economic Transformation of Spain and Portugal* (New York: Praeger, 1978).

3. Javier Rupérez, "Diez Años de Política Exterior," in Rafael López Pintor and Javier Rupérez, eds., *Diez Años en la Vida de los Españoles* (Barcelona: Plaza & Jánes, 1986). See also, Howard Wiarda, ed., *The Iberian-Latin American Connection. Implications for U. S. Foreign Policy* (Boulder: Westview, 1986).

4. Leopoldo Calvo Sotelo, speech before the Chamber of Commerce, Barcelona, May 20, 1987.

5. Rafael López Pintor, "Los cambios políticos," in López Pintor and Rupérez, eds., *Diez Años*; Emilio Rodriguez, "Contemporary Trends in Spain's Foreign Policy." Paper presented at the LASA Congress, March 1988.

6. Interview with José Pedro Perez Llorca, April 3, 1987.
7. Angel Viñas, "Spain, the United States, and NATO," in Christopher Abel and Nissa Torrents, eds., *Spain: Conditional Democracy* (London: St. Martin's Press, 1984).
8. Maravall, *Transition to Democracy*.
9. Rupérez, "Diez Años de Política Exterior."
10. Rafael López Pintor, chap. 3, in López Pintor, et al., *Los Partidos Conservadores y Demócrata Cristianos en España* (Madrid, n.p., 1985).
11. I am grateful to Julian Santamaría and Rosa Conde, directors of the CIS during the time I was in Spain, for facilitating my access to the rich mine of public opinion data there. Surveys of Spanish public opinion are now also being conducted by private firms, the most professional of which is OICOS. Their work is frequently published in *El País* and *Cambio 16*.
12. Maravall, chap. 12, lists the weaknesses of Spanish democracy as: the tensions between the central state and regionalism, persistent associative weakness of Spanish society and residual political cynicism, the current economic crisis, the context of social inequality, and terrorism and violence.

Index

ABC 30, 31, 34, 35, 36, 38, 39, 40
ACE Mobile Force 143
Alianza Popular (AP) 21, 26, 35, 56, 62, 162
Allende, Salvador 102, 103
Alliance for Progress 100
Arafat, Yasir 13, 134
Argentina 58, 62, 64, 109; Socialist Party of 98, 100, 103
Argueta, Manuel Colom 110
Ariane missiles 87
Arias Navarro, Carlos 60
Atlanticism 55–57, 61, 63, 66–68
Azores 128, 137

Bad Godesberg program 101
Balearic Islands 3. *See also* Spain, army deployment in Balearic and Canary Islands, Ceuta, Melilla
Barre, Raymond 77, 79
Basque terrorism 72, 77, 78, 80, 83, 84, 87–89, 125, 155
Bay of Biscay 72, 87
Belgium 130
Belize 95
Bolivian Movimiento Nationalista Revolutionarro (MNR) 100
Boyer, Miguel 65, 66
Brandt, Willy 105, 107
Brazil 99, 100, 107; Movimento Democrático Brasileiro (MDB) 104
Bush, George 26

Calvo Sotelo, Leopoldo 6, 14, 20, 21, 58, 80; North Atlanticism of 60–63; views on NATO 165–167
Cambio 16 30, 34, 35, 38, 39, 40
Canary Islands 3. *See also* Spain, army deployment in Balearic and Canary Islands, Ceuta, Melilla
Carrero Blanco, Luis 13
Central American crisis 4, 64, 95–97, 108–118
Centro de Estudios Democráticos de América Latina 109, 168
Centro de Investigaciones Sociológicas (CIS) 5, 161, 165
Ceuta 3, 15, 63, 134–136, 147. *See also* Spain, army deployment in Balearic and Canary Islands, Ceuta, Melilla
CGE-ITT 87
Chile 99, 102, 103, 109; Popular Socialist Party of 100
China 43
Chirac, Jacques 75, 76, 86–88
Church Commission 103
Cinco Días 34, 38
Coalición Popular 66
Colombia 112; Popular Socialist Party of 100
Common Market 16, 74, 84, 123, 125. *See also* European Economic Community (EC)
Communism 2, 12, 46, 59, 61, 75, 98, 100
Community of Twelve 56. *See also* European Economic Community

173

(EC)
Confederación Española de Organizaciones Empresariales (CEOE) 74
Conference on European Security 14
Contadora 68, 112, 117
Costa Rica 101, 110–112; Partido Liberación Nacional of 100, 109, 110
Cruz, Arturo 118
Cuba; 26th of July Movement 100; missile crisis 49, 127; revolution 100, 109, 117; Socialist Federation of 100; Spain's relations with 135

De Areilza, José 60, 69
De Carvajal, José Federico 16
Debré, Michel 75
Defense Planning Committee 143
Denmark 31, 111, 145, 146
Diario 16 30, 32, 34–36, 38–40
Dominican Republic 58, 104, 109; United Front of 100
Dumas, Roland 86

Eagleburger, Warren 117
East-West relations 63, 82, 105, 108, 114, 115, 160, 164, 169
Ebert Foundation 109, 112
Ecuador 100
Eisenhower administration 126
El Alcázar 30
El Correo Catalán 34
El Noticiero Universal 34
El País 24, 30–32, 34, 35, 37–40
El Periódico 30, 31, 34, 36, 38, 40
El Salvador 110, 111, 113, 116; civil war 111; Democratic Left of 110; Duarte government of 118; FDR-FMLN of 111; Movimiento Nacionalista Revolucionario (MNR) of 104
Época 35, 36, 39, 40
Equipo de Sociologia Electoral 20, 25
ETA (Euskadi Ta Askatasuna) 73
Euromissile 82, 144

European Christian Democratic parties 118
European Economic Community (EC) 8, 13, 15, 52, 57, 116, 134, 135, 137, 145, 154, 155, 159, 160, 162; Common Agricultural Policy (CAP) 76, 79; Council of Ministers of 79, 82, 84, 85; Fontainebleau summit 84; relationship to NATO 122–126; role in French-Spanish relations 73–78, 80–84, 86, 88, 89; Spain's entry into 63, 65, 66, 148; Stuttgart Formula 82
European Social Democrats 7, 61, 97, 99–104, 107–119
Europeanism 56, 66–68

F-23. *See* Spain, attempted military coup
Falkland Islands (Malvinas) 31, 62
Fidelistas 164
Ford administration 106
Fraga, Manuel 35, 56
France 7, 15, 42–45, 49, 55, 60, 63, 101, 111, 116; cooperation with Spain 74–80, 82–90; Paris 72, 83, 88, 89; Rambouillet 84; Rassemblement pour la République (RPR) 75. *See also* Gaullist; role in EC and NATO 123, 124, 129, 130, 135, 137, 141, 144, 146–148, 151, 154, 155, 159; Socialist Party of 75, 111, 116
Franco, Francisco 1–3, 6, 7, 12, 13, 17, 72, 76, 80, 134, 135, 149; Europeanism of 56, 58–60, 63, 68; legacy of 161, 163, 165, 168, 170; negotiations with United States 126–128, 131
François-Poncet, Jean 75, 78
Fédération Nationale des Syndicats d'Exploitants Agricoles (FNSEA) 76

Gaceta del Norte 31
Gaullist 3, 75, 146, 155, 160
Germany 2, 15, 55, 61, 68, 80, 82, 86,

101, 105, 116, 118, 152, 154, 159;
Bundestag Commission 21;
relations with Spain 42–44, 49;
role in NATO and EC 129, 130, 135,
141–143, 146, 151, 152, 154;
ostpolitik 101;
Sozialdemokratische Partei
Deutschlands (SPD) 101
Ghioldi, Américo 103
Gibraltar 3, 15, 18, 48, 55, 60, 63, 67,
124, 125, 127, 135, 147, 148
Giscard d'Estaing, Valéry 76–79, 123,
124
González, Felipe 5, 6, 20, 25, 28, 34,
92, 144, 161, 163, 170; decálogo of
65, 125; negotiations with France
81–84, 87; support for nonalignment 13, 15, 16; views on
NATO and EC 55–58, 62, 64–67, 69,
122, 124–128, 132, 133, 135
Grabendorff, Wolf 114, 121
Great Britain 44, 67, 95, 101, 116, 159,
165; relations with Latin America
60–63; role in NATO and EC 129,
130, 135, 142, 146, 151, 154
Greece 3, 25, 31, 34, 38, 55, 75, 89;
role in NATO and EC 111, 123,
127, 133, 137, 142, 146, 147, 151
Grupo Mixto 26, 27
Guatemala 109
Guerra, Alfonso 56, 64, 65
Guillaume, François 86
Gutiérrez Mellado, Manuel 131

Hermes space project 87
Hispanidad 2

ICBMs 51
IBERLANT 142
Instituto de Cooperación
Iberoamericana (ICI) 5, 9, 65
Interviú 30, 35, 40
Iranian crisis 128, 149
Israel 87, 128, 134, 149
Italy 2, 21, 86, 89; Aviano 127; role in
NATO and EC 123, 127–130, 142,
151

Jamaican Socialist Party 100
Japan 45, 105
JEMAD 132
JUJEM 132

King Juan Carlos I 60, 73, 76, 79, 83,
86
Kohl, Helmut 26, 82

La Granja Palace seminar 83
La Vanguardia 30, 32, 34–36, 38, 39,
40
Latin America 6, 7, 31, 135, 163, 164,
169; influence of European Social
Democrats on 95, 96, 98, 100–104,
107–109, 113–117; relations with
Spain 3, 4, 56, 57, 60–68, 83, 130,
134, 135, 159, 163; role in French-
Spanish cooperation 81, 84, 86, 89
Le Monde 83
Libya 149
Llopis, Rodolfo 12
Lluch, Ernest 65
Lomé convention 135
Low Countries 146
Lusinchi, Jaime 64
López Pintor, Rafael 168

Madrid 58, 64, 72, 73, 76, 77, 79, 80,
81, 83, 84, 86–89, 125–128, 130, 144,
169; 1953 Pact of 59
Maravall, José Maria 65, 162, 167
Marshall Plan 44
Marxism 105
Máximo 31–33, 37
Melilla 3, 15, 63, 134–136, 147. See
also Spain, army deployment in
Balearic and Canary Islands, Ceuta,
Melilla
META 131, 132
Mexico 100, 107, 112; Partido
Revolucionario Institutional (PRI)
of 104
Milans del Bosch, Jaime 79
Mitterrand, François 75, 79, 80–82,
84, 85, 87, 112, 144
Moncloa Pact 123, 167

Montevideo 100
Morocco 60, 87, 135, 136, 144, 147, 165
Morán, Fernando 16, 56, 63, 64, 66, 70, 83, 92, 121, 161
Mundo Obrero 30

NATO; creation of 13, 42–44; European defense strategy of 44–46, 67, 152–155; free riding/ semi-alignment in 3, 6, 137, 140, 145–152, 155, 156; military integration of 57, 59, 67, 71, 89, 122, 125, 133, 135, 136, 140, 145–147; relationship to EC, *see* European Economic Community (EC), relationship to NATO; Spain's integration into 12–19, 22–29, 32, 33, 42–52, 58–63, 80, 81, 132, 140–145; Spain's referendum on membership in 5, 6, 16–18, 20, 21, 23–29, 31, 34–38, 40, 50, 55, 56, 62–67, 71, 81, 82, 122, 125, 128, 140, 143, 164, 166; U.S. bases issue, *see* United States, bases
Netherlands 111
Nicaragua 114; conflict with Costa Rica 110; Contras 112, 118; Gulf of Fonseca 112; Sandinista National Liberation Front 64, 96, 104, 108–111, 116, 118, 164; Somoza government 109, 110
Nixon administration 106
Norway 31, 145, 146, 148
Nuclear weapons 13, 23, 24, 31, 71, 87, 89, 90, 126, 127, 137; role in NATO 39, 45–48, 50, 51, 140, 141, 143–147, 150–152, 159
Nunn amendment 153

Onega, F. 38
Oneto, J. 38
Ordóñez, Francisco Fernández 58, 66
Oreja, Marcelino 78, 124
Orvik, Nils 145, 148

Palestine Liberation Organization 134
Palme, Olof 107
Panama 100, 112
Paraguay 101, 109; Partido Revolucionario Febrerista of 100
Partido Comunista Español (PCE) 27, 59, 61, 66, 123, 131
Partido Democrático Popular (PDP) 162
Partido Socialista Obrero Español (PSOE) 6, 7, 21–23, 25–27, 81, 82, 116, 161, 162, 164–167, 169, 170; media manipulation by 29, 31, 38; views on NATO 13–18, 55–59, 61–68, 122–125, 128, 130, 131, 133, 134, 140, 147, 148, 155, 156
Pascua Militar 23
Pearce, Jenny 106
Persian Gulf 128; Alianza Popular Revolucionaria Americana (APRA) of 100
Portugal 11, 25, 31, 42, 56, 58, 60, 63, 75, 76, 79, 84, 89, 102; role in NATO and EC 123, 126, 133, 136, 142, 144
Pradera, J. 35
Prieto, Indalecio 12
Pueblo 30
Pérez Llorca, José Pedro 34, 61, 126, 135, 165–167

Reagan administration 4, 96, 97, 108, 112, 114, 117, 118, 153
Reykjavik 144, 154
Rupérez, Javier 13, 14, 19, 124, 167

SLBMs 51
Sahagun, Rodriguez 14
Saudi Arabia 128
Schori, Pierre 112, 113
Schultz, George 4, 160, 169
Sebastián, P. 35
SER 35, 36, 39, 40
Serra, Narciso 58, 65
Sicily 137
Socialist International 64, 97; influence on Latin America 99–

101, 103–105, 109, 110, 117
Solana, Javier 65
Soviet Union 2, 3, 59, 96, 98, 115, 133, 159, 161, 168; European perception of 42–47, 49, 144–149, 152
Spain; 1982 elections 22, 56, 62, 63, 111, 124; 1984 Defense Law 132; anti-Americanism in 2, 19, 146, 147, 149, 156, 163, 167, 168; armed forces 11, 12, 15, 23, 24, 48, 130, 132, 143, 142; army deployment in Balearic and Canary Islands, Ceuta, Melilla 129, 132, 134, 142; attempted military coup 79, 80, 124; Civil War 2, 43, 131, 161, 163; Congress of Deputies of 23, 62, 65, 66; Constitutional Tribunal of 23, 24; denuclearization mandate of 15, 18, 47; First Constitutional Legislature of 20; historical experience; public opinion in 1, 16, 23, 39, 41, 46, 74, 161, 165, 167, 168; referendum on membership in NATO, see NATO, Spain's referendum on membership in; relations with Arab World 87, 89, 134, 135, 149, 163; relations with Latin America, see Latin America, relations with Spain; relations with United States, see United States, relations with Spain; Right parties of 2, 3, 6, 17, 22, 26–28, 35, 78, 126, 156, 161–163, 168; tradition of neutrality 12, 31, 56, 61, 137; transition to democracy 11–13, 20–26, 34, 38, 60–63, 75, 77–81, 84, 85, 88, 122, 123, 131–33, 143, 155, 156, 161, 157, 170
Strauss, Franz Josef 26
Suárez, Adolfo 6, 13, 14, 125, 163, 164, 167; negotiations with France 77–79; role in Spain's transition to democracy 60, 61, 63, 64, 67; *tercermundismo* 56, 61, 63, 64; views on NATO 131, 134, 135
Syria 87

Tejero, Antoñio 34, 79
Third World 33, 43, 83, 135, 149, 153, 164
Tiempo 32, 35, 40
Truman administration 59
Tunisia 87
Turkey 3, 34, 39, 128, 129, 143, 144, 146, 147, 151; Incirlik 127
TVE 33, 38, 39, 40

United States; Bases 1, 2, 4, 13, 124, 141, 159, 161, 162, 168; at Morón 59, 67, 127, 128; at Rota 59, 67, 127; at Torrejón 4, 58, 59, 67, 127, 144, 169; at Zaragoza 58, 59, 67, 127, 128; relations with Spain 15, 41–44, 48, 50, 51, 56–61, 64, 67, 68, 71, 89, 126–144, 146–156; Strategic Defense Initiative 144; treaties with Spain 2, 43, 50, 59, 67, 127, 140, 160
Union pour la Démocratie Francaise (UDF) 75
United Nations 2, 58, 59, 108, 111
Unión del Centro Democrático (UCD) 14, 29, 58, 79, 123, 128, 148, 162
Uruguay 100, 109; Socialist party of 98

Venezuela 64, 101, 107, 112; Acción Democrática of 100, 110
Viñas, Angel 16, 17, 19, 28, 138, 165, 166

Warsaw Pact 49, 150
Weinberger, Caspar 4, 169
West European Union (WEU) 88, 89, 90, 137, 154
Whitehead, Laurence 104
World War I 39, 98, 99
World War II 1, 17, 39, 42, 44, 45, 49, 58, 95, 129, 137, 142

Ya 30, 31, 34, 36, 38, 39
Yom Kippur war 149
Yáñez, Luís 65

ZETA group 30, 35

About the Book and the Editors

Spain's entry into NATO has changed the strategic balance of the entire Western Alliance. It also has created considerable tension within the alliance and in Spanish domestic politics. Because it was kept out of European politics for so many years during the dictatorship of Franco, Spain's people and their leaders have perspectives on world issues that differ markedly from those of their European and U.S. counterparts. The roots of Spanish foreign-policy behavior lie deep in the material of Spanish history and politics.

Addressing this important topic, Spaniards of differing political viewpoints describe the nature of Spanish foreign-policy thinking and the effects of Spain's singular history on the nation's modern role in world affairs. Their chapters are juxtaposed to academic analyses of the consequences for the Western Alliance of Spain's entry into NATO, placing the Spanish perspective in a broader context and indicating with candor and clarity the points of tension between Spain and the other Western allies. The result is a comprehensive discussion—the first in English—of the problems presented by Spain's entry into NATO and a theoretical framework within which these problems can be analyzed.

Federico G. Gil is Kenan Professor of Political Science, Emeritus, at the University of North Carolina at Chapel Hill.

Joseph S. Tulchin is professor of history and director of the Office of International Programs at the University of North Carolina at Chapel Hill.

OCT 0 9 1990